First Certificate STAR

Practice Book

Grammar and Vocabulary

Luke Prodromou

Heinemann English Language Teaching, Oxford

A division of Macmillan Publishers Limited

Companies and representatives throughout the world

ISBN 0 435 28146 1
0 435 28152 6 (with key)

First published 1998

Designed by Robert Wheeler
Cover photograph by Maggie Milner

The author would like to thank Katy Wright and Jill Florent.

Printed and bound in Great Britain by Redwood Books, Trowbridge, Wiltshire

98 99 00 01 02 10 9 8 7 6 5 4 3 2 1

Contents

1 Yabba dabba doo

GRAMMAR AND USE OF ENGLISH

Exam practice: Use of English, Part 1

1 For questions 1–15, read the text below and decide which answer A, B, C or D best fits each space.

Walt Disney

There is no one who has not heard of Walt Disney; he is without (0) __B__ one of the most famous figures in the twentieth century and (1) ________ most people know hardly anything about him. (2) ________ he became one of the most successful men in history, he (3) ________ school at the age of sixteen and then studied art for a short time. By the (4) ________ years of this century, he had (5) ________ started to produce cartoons in Hollywood in (6) ________ with his brother Roy, who, for some reason, never (7) ________ to become as famous as Walt. Disney is perhaps most well known on (8) ________ of his lovable cartoon character, Mickey Mouse, who first (9) ________ in 1928 in a film called *Steamboat Willie*. One of the most (10) ________ cartoon films of all time is *Snow White and the Seven Dwarfs*, which, when it was (11) ________ in 1937, was the first full-length cartoon in the history of the cinema.

(12) ________ the 1950s, Walt Disney had become one of the world's major (13) ________ of films for cinema and television. As Disney Productions (14) ________ , its founder retained complete artistic control of the films and he also (15) ________ on to publish books for children and cartoon strips in newspapers, featuring such characters as Donald Duck and Pluto the dog.

	A	B	C	D
0	A comparison	B doubt	C disagreement	D explanation
1	A yet	B then	C already	D however
2	A Despite	B In spite of	C Although	D Even
3	A graduated	B completed	C left	D failed
4	A primary	B early	C beginning	D initial
5	A still	B soon	C yet	D already
6	A partnership	B friendship	C relationship	D membership
7	A achieved	B reached	C succeeded	D managed
8	A case	B account	C view	D regard
9	A appeared	B performed	C starred	D began
10	A common	B excited	C popular	D known
11	A seen	B released	C circulated	D advertised
12	A Until	B Since	C By	D To
13	A businessmen	B owners	C publishers	D producers
14	A grew	B enlarged	C increased	D succeeded
15	A took	B put	C pushed	D went

Exam practice: Use of English, Part 4

2 For questions 1–15, read the text below and look carefully at each line. Some of the lines are correct, and some have a word which should not be there. If a line is correct, put a tick (✓). If a line has a word which should not be there, write the word.

Duck Tales: The Movie

the 0 Viewers who enjoy the Disney's famous cartoon
✓ 00 characters will enjoy *Duck Tales: The Movie*. This new
________ 1 Disney production is a great movie for to take the kids to
________ 2 during all the holidays. In spite of a few hostile reviews,
________ 3 audiences up and down the country have been queuing
________ 4 up to see it. In it stars some of Disney's most popular
________ 5 creations: Uncle Scrooge and his crazy nephews Huey,
________ 6 Dewey and Louie. After years of searching, stingy Uncle
________ 7 Scrooge has at last discovers the fabulous lost treasure
________ 8 of the legendary thief, Collie Baba. But when the treasure
________ 9 slips through his fingers and Scrooge comes back home
________ 10 empty-handed, except for an old lamp in which, of course,
________ 11 contains a magic Genie. Scrooge's nephews will try to
________ 12 change their lives as they come up with more and more
________ 13 things for the Genie to do. However, the evil Merlock also
________ 14 wants to get hold of the lamp. Sparks fly away as Merlock
________ 15 does everything he can to steal the Genie.

Exam practice: Use of English, Part 5

3 For questions 1–10, read the text below. Use the word given in capitals at the end of each line to form a word that fits in the space in the same line.

Fame and fortune

Macaulay Culkin, now a (0) *youthful* twenty year old, became — YOUTH
one of the most (1) ________________ and well-paid stars in Hollywood — FAME
while he was still an (2) ________________ . Now he has grown up, he — ADOLESCENCE
can look back on a (3) ________________ which reads like a fairy-tale. — CHILD
There are indeed few American children who can claim to have
been the most famous child in the world. This was the case with
Culkin after his (4) ________________ in *Home Alone* in 1986. — APPEAR
Although this film made him a (5) ________________ name, his first — HOUSE
(6) ________________ movie had come a couple of years earlier when — SUCCESS
his (7) ________________ in *Rocket Gibraltar* earned him very — PERFORM
(8) ________________ reviews from the critics, who are not noted for — FAVOUR
their (9) ________________ towards child stars. Culkin's career did not — KIND
end with *Home Alone*. As a (10) ________________ he went on to — TEEN
appear in a number of more serious films.

Tense review

Exam practice: Use of English, Part 3

4 For questions 1–10, complete the second sentence so that it has a similar meaning to the first sentence, using the word given. Do not change the word given. You must use between two and five words, including the word given.

0 My sister is not old enough to ride a bicycle.
too
My sister is ___*too young to*___ ride a bicycle.

1 A knock at the door interrupted Dad's story.
telling
Dad ______________________ when there was a knock at the door.

2 The Oscar ceremony is on television live tonight at eight o'clock.
broadcasting
They ______________________ live at eight o'clock tonight.

3 I was approached by a stranger who asked me the way.
up
A stranger ______________________ and asked me the way.

4 The total sales for this video are already over a million.
sold
This video ______________________ copies already.

5 He hasn't stopped talking since he came into the room.
been
He ______________________ the moment he came into the room.

6 Seeing a cartoon for the first time was an exciting experience.
seen
I ______________________ before so it was an exciting experience.

7 What did she have on at the party?
was
What ______________________ at the party?

8 After sitting in front of the computer all evening I felt sleepy.
been
I felt sleepy because ______________________ in front of the computer all evening.

9 I agree to write the report if you give me the information.
will
Give me the information ______________________ the report.

10 The programme only finished a minute ago.
just
The programme ______________________ finished.

5 Complete this text using the correct form of the verbs in brackets.

Wonderkids

Infant prodigies in the cinema have been with us a long time. The older generation still (1) ____________________ (remember) Shirley Temple, Mickey Rooney and Judy Garland. Some of these talented child stars (2) ____________________ (go) on to shake off the 'wonderkid' label later in life and (3) ____________________ (manage) to become successful adult actors. Others, on the other hand, (4) ____________________ (continue) to appear in films but with very little of the success they (5) ____________________ (have) as children. Sadly, the majority of them (6) ____________________ (disappear) soon after their first appearance and cinema-goers (7) ____________________ (not/see) them since.

Our own generation (8) ____________________ (also/produce) its fair share of child stars or 'superbrats', as some movie magazines (9) ____________________ (refer) to them. These young stars (10) ____________________ (make) not only a name for themselves but also a lot of money. In recent years on the big screen we (11) ____________________ (see) Lukas Haas play the boy who (12) ____________________ (witness) a murder in the film *Witness*. He (13) ____________________ (make) other movies since then, but he (14) ____________________ (not/become) a big name in Hollywood. The most famous of the superbrats is undoubtedly Macaulay Culkin who (15) ____________________ (earn) as much as, if not more than, the most expensive superstars in Hollywood.

6 Choose the correct tense in these sentences.

1 I can't come out now because I finish/I'm finishing my homework.
2 You've dropped your wallet. I'll/I'm going to pick it up for you.
3 They awarded/They've awarded Bob Crews the Oscar; it was on the news just now.
4 They were broadcasting/They broadcast the match live when rain stopped play.
5 Can you remember what you were wearing/you wore the night you lost your wallet?
6 I went/I had been skiing before but last week was still a real challenge!
7 I've read/I've been reading a new thriller by Stephen King. It's so good I can't put it down.
8 I had been waiting/I had waited for ages for her to write before finally the letter arrived.
9 When I will finish/I have finished reading this book, I'm going to read another one by him.
10 OK, I'm going now but I'll see/I'm seeing you at the same time tomorrow.

7 Complete these sentences using the correct form of the verbs in brackets.

1 They ____________________ (broadcast) the programme on TV twice already.
2 TV chat shows ____________________ (increase) in number all the time.
3 It was the first time the actor ____________________ (receive) such bad reviews.
4 I ____________________ (watch) my favourite soap opera when the doorbell ____________________ (ring).
5 I ____________________ (watch) TV for hours – I've had enough!
6 I usually ____________________ (tell) the kids a story before bedtime.
7 I ____________________ (go) to an exhibition of modern art last week.
8 As it ____________________ (snow) all night the roads were blocked.
9 The most popular film he ____________________ (make) so far is *Riding High*.
10 We looked out of the window and saw it ____________________ (rain) so we stayed in.

VOCABULARY

Word formation

1 Complete this table.

verb	adjective	noun
popularize	popular	
invent		1 2
		1 producer 2
	famous	
		1 creation 2
respond		responsive
decide		
		suburb
	pleasant	
prepare		
		nature
originate		origin
	historic/al	
appear		
employ		1 employer 2 3
translate		1 2

2 Complete these sentences using one of the words from the table above in each space.

1 Would you like to live in the centre of town or in the ________________ ?
2 He ________________ to be very serious, but in fact he has a great sense of humour.
3 She is ________________ now, but she was out of work for over a year.
4 Tourists to Barcelona can visit a great number of ________________ monuments.
5 Can you ________________ this letter from English into Italian?
6 The Indians were the ________________ inhabitants of America.
7 My country ________________ olives and citrus fruits and exports them to other countries.
8 What would you say is the most ________________ TV programme in your country?
9 When you have a party, you have to do a lot of ________________ beforehand.
10 The ________________ of the telephone revolutionized communication between people.

Phrasal verbs

3 Replace the underlined words in these sentences with the correct form of one of the phrasal verbs below. Make any other changes that are necessary. Use two of the phrasal verbs twice.

make up	take up	look up	come up	come up with	draw up
put up	put up with	hold up	go up	give up	

1 If you can't think of a funny story that really happened, then you can invent one.

If you can't come up with a funny story that really happened, then you can make one up.

2 On Saturday morning I usually sit down and make a list of all the things I have to do, then something happens unexpectedly and I end up only doing half of them.

____

3 She started going to German classes but found the language difficult and soon stopped going.

____

4 In the Use of English paper, the same questions are set again and again.

____

5 I hate reading a book in English if I have to check every new word in the dictionary.

____

6 One way to get a lot of money is to rob a bank, but I wouldn't recommend it.

____

7 I won't have to stay in a hotel in London because a friend has offered to let me stay for the night.

____

8 How can you stand all that noise from next door?

____

9 Sorry I'm late. I was delayed at the post office – there was a huge queue.

____

10 Inflation increased by 2.5% last year.

____

2 In good company

GRAMMAR AND USE OF ENGLISH

Exam practice: Use of English, Part 1

1 For questions 1–15, read the text below and decide which answer A, B, C or D best fits each space.

Are you the person you'd like to be?

Have you ever regretted doing something you shouldn't have done or something you didn't do which you should have? At one (0) ___C___ or another we probably all have. There's no (1) ________ in getting depressed about it now – it's no (2) ________ crying over spilt milk. However, there may be some (3) ________ in thinking about exactly what happened and why because we might be able to (4) ________ some conclusions for the future.

One thing we all do now and again is to lose our (5) ________ with a friend or close (6) ________ . The odd thing is that we more often display great anger (7) ________ someone we're (8) ________ of than towards strangers. The explanation may be that we see friends and relatives as a kind of safety net, an opportunity to let off a bit of steam in a safe (9) ________ , whereas the (10) ________ of insulting a stranger or a (11) ________ at work could be far more serious.

Being honest is usually (12) ________ of as a virtue and undoubtedly this is the (13) ________ . On the other hand, we have all experienced occasions when we have spoken our minds to someone, (14) ________ them exactly what we feel, and then have found ourselves (15) ________ with feelings of guilt and remorse. Perhaps we should have kept our mouths shut?

	A	B	C	D
0	A occasion	B hour	C time	D day
1	A reason	B purpose	C point	D advantage
2	A use	B point	C value	D benefit
3	A gain	B profit	C goodness	D worth
4	A draw	B make	C do	D take
5	A temper	B mind	C anger	D head
6	A relationship	B member	C familiar	D relative
7	A at	B with	C towards	D about
8	A keen	B fond	C friendly	D familiar
9	A circle	B area	C surroundings	D environment
10	A effect	B consequences	C conclusion	D punishment
11	A staff	B mate	C professional	D colleague
12	A thought	B considered	C regarded	D believed
13	A true	B case	C event	D fact
14	A telling	B saying	C speaking	D describing
15	A full	B heavy	C sad	D overcome

Exam practice: Use of English, Part 2

2 For questions 1–15, read the text below and think of the word which best fits each space. Use only one word in each space. After each space you are given a clue to the kind of word that is missing.

Regrets

Most of us (0) ___are___ (auxiliary verb) always forgetting important dates, apart (1) __________ (preposition) the lucky few (2) __________ (relative pronoun) are blessed with a good memory or the ability to organize (3) __________ (reflexive pronoun) so they don't forget important obligations. How many times (4) __________ (auxiliary verb) we all said, 'I wish I had remembered!' How (5) __________ (adverb of frequency) have we offended people by failing to remember (6) __________ (pronoun) birthdays or name days? (7) __________ (conjunction) they say it doesn't matter, we know, deep down, that we (8) __________ (auxiliary verb) hurt their feelings. We can always try to make it (9) __________ (preposition) to them next time but unfortunately the damage has (10) __________ (auxiliary verb) done and our relationship with that person (11) __________ (modal verb, future) never quite be the same again.

On the other hand, we sometimes do (12) __________ (*very* or *too*?) much for someone else because we want to please them and then feel we have damaged (13) __________ (pronoun) own interests in so doing. When friends (14) __________ (auxiliary verb) involved we may find it difficult to say 'no' when they ask us to (15) __________ (*do* or *make*?) them a favour, but true friendship should mean that we can say 'no' without risk to the relationship.

Exam practice: Use of English, Part 4

3 For questions 1–15, read the text below and look carefully at each line. Some of the lines are correct, and some have a word which should not be there. If a line is correct, put a tick (✓). If a line has a word which should not be there, write the word.

Positive thinking

___to___ 0 Positive thinking does not mean you to have to find every
___✓___ 00 idea absolutely wonderful. It does mean you have to be
________ 1 ready to explore an idea and to try and bring out whatever
________ 2 good features it may has. The next step might be to find
________ 3 the weaknesses in case the idea and to try and strengthen
________ 4 them, rather than for using them simply as an excuse for
________ 5 rejecting the whole idea. Finally, the idea, after it has
________ 6 been explored, may not be used up because there is a
________ 7 better one or because, good though it is, it is not the suitable.
________ 8 There is nothing wrong with being positive about an idea
________ 9 at first and then rejecting it later, when you can see that
________ 10 it won't to work. It is easy to be negative and critical and
________ 11 it is time we had showed less respect for this kind of
________ 12 destructive thinking and emphasized on creative thinking
________ 13 more. We should first make ourselves list the positive things
________ 14 about an idea before we criticize it. Too much talent is wasted
________ 15 in the negative thinking. So remember – think positive!

Exam practice: Use of English, Part 5

4 For questions 1–10, read the text below. Use the word given in capitals at the end of each line to form a word that fits in the space in the same line.

My ideal job

One thing I know is that I wouldn't like to have an (0) *occupation*	OCCUPY
that has anything to do with physics, (1) ________________ or maths;	CHEMIST
I am not the (2) ________________ type at all. In fact, at school I was a	SCIENCE
complete (3) ________________ in these subjects. Neither am I very	FAIL
good at dealing with people, nor am I (4) ________________ , so jobs in	AMBITION
business, administration and (5) ________________ don't really interest	MANAGE
me either. Moreover, I find it (6) ________________ to be surrounded by	IRRITATE
a lot of people; I would much rather have a job involving creative	
work or (7) ________________ skills of some sort. I'd like to have the	ART
chance to work outdoors (8) ________________ and perhaps do a bit of	OCCASION
travelling too. I am not (9) ________________ concerned about becoming	PARTICULAR
rich but I would like to have a (10) ________________ income – enough	REASON
to live comfortably.	

Questions and question tags

5 Complete the questions in the questionnaires below, then choose one of the questionnaires and write your own answers.

You and clothes

1 *Do* you dress before breakfast or after?

I usually dress before breakfast.

2 ________________ you wear the same kind of clothes five years ago as you do today?

____

3 ________________ someone else buy your clothes for you?

____

4 ________________ you ever bought anything and then not worn it?

____

5 ________________ you fashion conscious?

____

6 ________________ does it take you to get dressed in the morning?

____

7 ________________ do you wear when you go to a party?

____

8 ________________ pairs of shoes do you have?

____

Your best friend

1 ______________ has this person been your best friend?

____

2 ______________ were you when you first met? At school, work or somewhere else?

____

3 ______________ your friend born in the same year as you?

____

4 ______________ quality do you like most in your best friend?

____

5 ______________ your friend's personality similar or different to yours?

____

6 ______________ does most of the talking, you or your friend?

____

7 ______________ you ever argue with your friend? What about?

____

8 ______________ you ever lent your friend any money?

____

6 Complete these questions with a tag.

1 You couldn't lend me some money, *could you* ?
2 You've always lived in the same house, ______________ ?
3 You wouldn't refuse to give a beggar money, ______________ ?
4 You like classical music, ______________ ?
5 You don't mind people gossiping about you, ______________ ?
6 You'd never steal anything, ______________ ?
7 You used to have a different hair style, ______________ ?
8 You'd better work harder, ______________ ?
9 They don't dislike you, ______________ ?
10 Let's go to an opera this evening, ______________ ?

Giving advice

7 Give advice on these problems by finishing the sentences below.

1 My boyfriend says he wants us to split up.
If I were you, *I'd talk to him and try to find out why.*

2 I'm hopeless at maths and I need to do well at it.
The best thing to do ______________________________

3 I can't keep my weight down.
Why don't you try ______________________________

4 Our neighbours are incredibly noisy.
I suggest you ______

5 I'm always broke.
I suggest ______

6 My boss says I don't work hard enough.
Don't you think ______

7 No one ever writes me letters.
You could try ______

8 I can't get up in time to go to work.
You should ______

8 Complete these sentences with an appropriate expression for giving advice. Then match the sentences with the problems in exercise 7.

1 *If I were you,* I would threaten to call the police.
2 ______ writing to them first or giving them a ring.
3 ______ eating what you like and not worrying about your weight.
4 ______ is ask someone to give you private lessons.
5 ______ get yourself a new alarm clock.
6 ______ finding a job that pays more.
7 ______ look around for someone else.
8 ______ is get to work earlier and leave a bit later.

VOCABULARY

Word formation

1 Complete this table. Sometimes there is more than one possible adjective.

noun	adjective	noun	adjective
society	*sociable, social*	amusement	
disgust		influence	
irritation		despair	
misery		care	
skill		favour	
importance		practice	
attention		accuracy	
interest		nature	
communication		worry	
gratitude		boredom	

2 Complete these sentences using one of the adjectives from the table in exercise 1 in each space.

1 He has a lot of power in the office. He is very *influential* .
2 She has to go to hospital to have a serious operation. She feels ________ .
3 No one takes an interest in the teacher's lesson. The teacher is ________ ; the students are ________ .
4 She is very good at fixing things around the house. She is ________ .
5 People are born, they grow up and eventually they die; just like the leaves on a tree. It's ________ .
6 They are the pop group I like best. They are my ________ .
7 She tells some really great jokes. She is ________ .
8 She drives slowly and always looks in the mirror. She is a ________ driver.
9 She sent me a present after I helped her to pass the exam. She feels ________ to me.
10 Students should listen to what the teacher is saying in class. They should be ________ .

Phrasal verbs

3 Complete these dialogues using the correct form of one of the phrasal verbs below in each space.

hold on	take on	get on	count on	go on	put on	turn on
leave on	try on	put through	let down	take up	set up	

A: Hello, can you (1) *put* me *through* to Jane Smith, please?
B: Yes, (2) ________ a moment, sir ... I'm afraid she's out at the moment. Can I take a message?
A: I'd rather send a fax, if you don't mind (3) ________ it ________ .

A: I'm pleased to tell you we have decided to (4) ________ you ________ as a sales manager.
B: Thanks, I hope I don't (5) ________ you ________ .
A: I'm sure you won't. We'd like you to (6) ________ your duties immediately, if possible.

A: If you want to (7) ________ in this company, you have to work hard.
B: I do. Don't worry, I won't let you down. You can (8) ________ me.
A: I'm sure ... now, let's (9) ________ with the letters. I don't think we've finished yet.

A: Do you think this pullover suits me?
B: Why don't you (10) ________ it ________ ?

A: The programme's finished. Shall I switch the TV off?
B: No, (11) ________ it ________ – I want to hear the news.

A: They're (12) ________ an exhibition of photographs at the Arts Centre.
B: Yes, the whole thing was (13) ________ by the local Arts Council.

3 The good, the bad and the unbearable

GRAMMAR AND USE OF ENGLISH

Exam practice: Use of English, Part 1

1 For questions 1–15, read the text below and decide which answer A, B, C or D best fits each space.

Lisbon: on the waterfront

The organizers of EXPO 1998 in Lisbon have a big (0) __A__ on their hands. They aim to (1) ________ on an international fair that will not only attract eight million visitors but will also (2) ________ back to life a large part of Lisbon's riverside and help (3) ________ the world's oceans. The Lisbon Fair will be a tribute to the five hundredth (4) ________ of the explorer Vasco da Gama's sea voyage to India. It will (5) ________ place at the same time as the United Nations' 'Year of the Oceans'.

The EXPO committee want to (6) ________ building an expensive four-month festival which will (7) ________ forever. Instead, they would like to give Lisbon something which will be around (8) ________ it is all over. It is clear that Lisbon has learnt from the (9) ________ of Seville's EXPO 1992, a successful (10) ________ which, however, left behind a desert of expensive but (11) ________ buildings.

The intended site of the EXPO is a five-mile stretch of river which (12) ________ people know about because it is occupied by out-dated industries that (13) ________ the environment. When the fair is over, an (14) ________ more than five times the size of EXPO's 60 hectares will provide property for (15) ________ and businesses in a city in which there is a lack of both.

0	A task	B work	C weight	D business
1	A take	B make	C put	D build
2	A come	B bring	C take	D make
3	A save	B keep	C repair	D restore
4	A celebration	B festival	C year	D anniversary
5	A take	B have	C make	D get
6	A deny	B avoid	C escape	D refuse
7	A destroy	B last	C take	D disappear
8	A afterwards	B after	C finally	D consequently
9	A fault	B mistakes	C slip	D false
10	A event	B fact	C show	D performance
11	A useful	B usual	C useless	D essential
12	A none	B any	C much	D few
13	A infect	B contain	C poison	D pollute
14	A territory	B place	C area	D district
15	A dwellers	B neighbours	C householders	D residents

Exam practice: Use of English, Part 4

2 For questions 1–15, read the text below and look carefully at each line. Some of the lines are correct, and some have a word which should not be there. If a line is correct, put a tick (✓). If a line has a word which should not be there, write the word.

Leave it at home

___✓___ 0 Cars became popular as a quick and comfortable way of getting
__*will*__ 00 around. This is still true when you will drive along a quiet country
________ 1 road or a modern motorway. As far as you getting from one place
________ 2 to another in the city is concerned, it is a different story. Whenever
________ 3 I want to get up anywhere in a hurry, I leave the car at home
________ 4 and go on foot. It often turns out to be much more quicker. I still make
________ 5 the mistake now and again of thinking the car is an efficient means
________ 6 of a transport. The other day my wife was feeling a bit under the
________ 7 weather. She had been having terrible headaches for some long
________ 8 time and she decided she couldn't take it anymore and asked from
________ 9 me to give her a lift to the doctor, whose surgery is in the centre
________ 10 part of town. We live in a suburb in the old quarter of the city and
________ 11 it is about twenty minutes away on foot. On the way back, however,
________ 12 it is all uphill and I must to admit it can be exhausting, especially on a
________ 13 hot day. Reluctantly I got the car out of the garage and we set it off,
________ 14 me muttering about the wonders of taxis. My heart was sank as we
________ 15 hit the first traffic jam – I knew we were beginning a long journey.

Exam practice: Use of English, Part 5

3 For questions 1–10, read the text below. Use the word given in capitals at the end of each line to form a word that fits in the space in the same line.

Far from the madding crowd?

We live in a new residential area on the outskirts of London. It is
a quiet (0) __*neighbourhood*__ , which makes a nice change after living NEIGHBOUR
in one of the noisiest (1) ________________ of London for many years. SUBURBAN
The house is set in beautiful (2) ________________ , though there is one SURROUND
fairly major (3) ________________ problem: a chemical factory about ENVIRONMENT
five miles away in the (4) ________________ zone. Unfortunately, INDUSTRY
the waste from the factory has caused serious (5) ________________ POLLUTE
of the atmosphere and the river. Another (6) ________________ is the ADVANTAGE
night life – there isn't any. If you want (7) ________________ , you have ENTERTAIN
to invent it yourself or drive into (8) ________________ London, with all CENTRE
the hassle of finding a (9) ________________ parking space. Luckily, it SUIT
is only five minutes walk from our house to the nearest
(10) ________________ station. GROUND

Present simple and present continuous

Exam practice: Use of English, Part 3

4 For questions 1–10, complete the second sentence so that it has a similar meaning to the first sentence, using the word given. Do not change the word given. You must use between two and five words, including the word given.

0 My sister is not old enough to ride a bicycle.
too
My sister is ____too young to____ ride a bicycle.

1 Trains are rarely late in my country.
time
Usually, trains ________________ in my country.

2 She never stops saying how much she dislikes public transport.
complaining
She ________________ about public transport.

3 My flatmate studies history.
share
I ________________ someone who is studying history.

4 My neighbour often plays loud music and it really irritates me.
always
My neighbour ________________ loud music and it really irritates me.

5 The bus service in our city becomes more inefficient every year.
getting
The bus service in our city ________________ and more inefficient.

6 That blouse and skirt are a perfect match.
goes
That blouse ________________ your skirt.

7 In the end, the motorway was a great success.
turned
The motorway ________________ a great success.

8 He is often in a bad mood.
rarely
He ________________ good mood.

9 My old teacher never fails to greet me when he sees me in the street.
'hello'
My old teacher ________________ when he sees me in the street.

10 You moan about the weather all the time and it gets on my nerves.
are
You ________________ about the weather.

5 Complete this text using the correct form (present simple or present continuous) of one of the verbs below in each space. Use one of the verbs twice.

lead	rain	begin	feel	write	stay	have
look	smell	sit	go	wish	take	hope

Dear Maria,

Hi! I (1) ___*am writing*___ to you from our nice, new country cottage in the village of Foxwood.
I (2) ______________ everything is well with you. I only (3) ______________ I could say the same about myself or about the life I (4) ______________ at the moment.
I think I told you my parents had bought this old, eighteenth century cottage because they (5) ______________ it is a good place to bring up kids. I suppose they (6) ______________ a point. I'm sure all this fresh air is doing me a lot of good and I suppose it only (7) ______________ an hour to get to the city centre from here. And, I have to admit, it's very pretty. As I write I (8) ______________ at the kitchen window, which (9) ______________ onto a lovely wood and I often (10) ______________ for walks there. It (11) ______________ right now so I can't go for my little stroll as I planned. The flowers (12) ______________ lovely this time of year.
So, in many ways, life is OK. On the other hand, there isn't much else to do here. It's so quiet and the peacefulness (13) ______________ to get on my nerves. At the moment a friend of mine from Spain (14) ______________ with us and that's great. Her name's Pilar and she comes from Pamplona. We (15) ______________ a great time together, but what am I going to do when she goes back home on Friday?

Lots of love,

Helen

6 The present simple is often used to tell jokes. Rewrite the jokes below, changing the tenses where appropriate.

1 This man was driving a big lorry along the high street. Suddenly he came to a corner and a small car that was coming up behind him crashed into the back of his lorry.
'Hey!' shouted the driver of the car. 'Why didn't you put your hand out to signal that you were going to turn right?'
'Are you crazy?' answered the lorry driver. 'What would have been the point of sticking my hand out?

This man is driving a big lorry along the high street.

____

____

____

2 A man was driving along a country road, admiring the beautiful scenery. Suddenly another car appeared round a bend in the road and the man just missed crashing into it. The window of the other car opened and the woman inside shouted 'Pig!' Very angry, the man opened his window and shouted back 'Cow!' But just as the man turned the corner …

____

____

____

____

3 A woman driver stopped at a red traffic light. Then the green light came on but she couldn't start her car. She tried again and again, but all in vain. Then the lights changed from red to orange and then back to green and back to red again. After a few minutes, a policeman came up to the woman and asked her ...

____

____

____

____

Now match the jokes with the appropriate last line below.

a 'What's up? Don't you like any of the colours?'

b If you couldn't see my lorry, how could you see my hand?'

c ... he crashes into a huge pig in the middle of the road.

VOCABULARY

Word formation

1 Complete this table.

verb	noun	verb	noun
choose	*choice*	govern	
compare		improve	
complain		pollute	
construct		predict	
develop		solve	

2 Match words from list A with words from list B to make compound nouns. Use one of the words in list A twice.

A	B	
under	cycle	*underground*
ring	hole	__________
motor	road	__________
side	ground	__________
pot	park	__________
car	way	__________
high		__________

3 Complete these sentences using one of the words from exercises 1 and 2 in each space.

1 Cars go at a much higher speed on the *motorway* .
2 The __________ has decided to call an election.
3 Most of the __________ in this town is caused by cars and factories.
4 If you have any __________ about the food, go and see the manager.
5 It's quite easy to __________ the weather nowadays using satellite information.
6 A __________ goes around a city and avoids traffic in the centre.
7 __________ of a new office block has begun in the centre of town.
8 They should repair the __________ in the road; they are very dangerous.
9 Is there no __________ to the problem of overcrowded cities?
10 As he was driving along the main street he suddenly turned into a little __________ .

Phrasal verbs

4 Match the phrasal verbs in list A with their meanings in list B. Four of the phrasal verbs have more than one meaning.

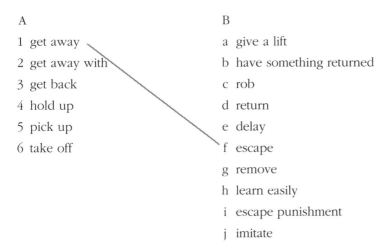

A	B
1 get away	a give a lift
2 get away with	b have something returned
3 get back	c rob
4 hold up	d return
5 pick up	e delay
6 take off	f escape
	g remove
	h learn easily
	i escape punishment
	j imitate

5 Complete these expressions using one of the phrasal verbs above.

1 *hold up* a bank
2 __________ home from a party
3 __________ the way someone talks
4 __________ a foreign language
5 __________ your pullover
6 __________ a hitch-hiker
7 __________ the traffic
8 __________ cheating in an exam
9 __________ something someone has borrowed
10 __________ from the police

4 Culture shock

GRAMMAR AND USE OF ENGLISH

Exam practice: Use of English, Part 2

1 For questions 1–15, read the text below and think of the word which best fits each space. Use only one word in each space. Use the articles *a* and *the* more than once.

A day in Spain

The morning in Spain lasts (0) ___until___ two o'clock, when it is time for lunch. After that there's (1) __________ siesta and the afternoon begins at about five o'clock. At eight o'clock people begin thinking about having (2) __________ drink and so the evening begins. Dinner is served from nine o'clock and the evening may continue well into the night.

There's no town, large or small, without (3) __________ main square and it is (4) __________ great public festivities take place. (5) __________ square is the heart of community life. In the past, the entrances to the square used to (6) __________ blocked so that it could serve as a bullring, something which is still done (7) __________ villages where they do not have their own bullring.

In the cities, bars are popular meeting places where one goes for (8) __________ aperitif at lunch-time, to drink a glass (9) __________ wine with friends and to try the *tapas*, which may be anything (10) __________ olives to seafood. After work comes the *tertulia* or informal club hour (11) __________ men gather and, (12) __________ a glass of wine, discuss (13) __________ news, politics and football or tell jokes. The end of the afternoon is (14) __________ people often have a cup of chocolate or, in summer, (15) __________ refreshing, cold drink and *churros*: delicious, twisted fritters.

Exam practice: Use of English, Part 4

2 For questions 1–15, read the text below and look carefully at each line. Some of the lines are correct, and some have a word which should not be there. If a line is correct, put a tick (✓). If a line has a word which should not be there, write the word.

An international summer camp

___of___ 0 For the last few of years, my children have been going to a summer camp
___✓___ 00 in northern Greece called Skouras Camp. They always seem to have a
________ 1 good time, so if you're wondering what to do with the kids for three
________ 2 weeks this summer, you could do worse than send them up to this
________ 3 beautiful camp on the shores of the Aegean Sea. If your children, like
________ 4 mine, are keen on adventure, sports and good company, the Skouras

________ 5 Camp will keep them busy all day doing the things they most enjoy them.
________ 6 Skouras is an international camp with our children from all over the
________ 7 world. My children have made friends with children of their own age from
________ 8 Poland, China, Denmark and the United States. Naturally they do get lots
________ 9 of opportunities to practise their English as English is the only language spoken.
________ 10 The Camp it is located in one of the most beautiful parts of Chalkidiki. It is
________ 11 and huge (120 000 square metres) and is just a stone's throw away from the clear,
________ 12 blue Aegean Sea. It takes the children just five minutes to walk to the golden,
________ 13 sandy beach on the foot. The programme is packed with exciting activities for
________ 14 children. Apart from the usual water sports, my kids' favourite activities are horse
________ 15 riding and table tennis. Other sports include basketball, volley-ball and athletics.
The Camp ends with a sports contest in the last week which all parents are invited to attend.

Exam practice: Use of English, Part 5

3 For questions 1–10, read the text below. Use the word given in capitals at the end of each line to form a word that fits in the space in the same line.

A tip round Europe

The British are (0) ___*considered*___ to be among the worst tippers in	CONSIDER
the world but is that because they simply don't know the rules?	
Customs differ between countries, so it is not (1) ________________	SURPRISE
that in Tokyo they do things (2) ________________ from London.	DIFFERENT
In British restaurants, for example, a tip is (3) ________________	GENERAL
included in the bill and this is the case in most (4) ________________	NORTH
European countries. In some Mediterranean countries, such as	
Greece and Spain, the customer is expected to pay a little extra	
for (5) ________________ service. As for bars and pubs, again customs	SATISFY
vary. In Britain, one (6) ________________ does not have to pay a tip in	CERTAIN
pubs, while in hotel bars it is (7) ________________ common to leave	FAIR
your small change behind. This is the case in (8) ________________ too,	GERMAN
but in France you leave a tip only when drinks are brought to your	
table. In the (9) ________________ of European countries, with the	MAJOR
(10) ________________ of Ireland where it applies only in top hotels,	EXCEPT
porters receive a tip for carrying your luggage to your room for you.	

Articles

Exam practice: Use of English, Part 3

4 For questions 1–10, complete the second sentence so that it has a similar meaning to the first sentence, using the word given. Do not change the word given. You must use between two and five words, including the word given.

0 My sister is not old enough to ride a bicycle.
too
My sister is _____too young to_____ ride a bicycle.

1 The name of my dog is Rover.
called
I've ________________________________ Rover.

2 Why don't we go to the cinema tonight?
film
Let's ________________________________ tonight.

3 One of my favourite pastimes is watching plays.
theatre
Going ________________________________ I really enjoy doing.

4 He became a prisoner five years ago.
prison
He ________________________________ for five years.

5 Italy is where we went for a holiday last year.
on
We went ________________________________ last year.

6 Americans are usually quite self-confident.
States
People ________________________________ are usually quite self-confident.

7 The medical profession is a difficult one.
doctor
Being ________________________________ easy.

8 John is still receiving treatment in the clinic.
hospital
John ________________________________ receiving treatment.

9 Children don't attend classes on Saturday.
school
Children don't ________________________________ on Saturday.

10 You can do a lot of things both day and night in Barcelona.
at
There is plenty to do during ________________________________ night in Barcelona.

5 Complete this text with *their, some, a, the* or Ø (when no article is needed). Sometimes there is more than one possibility.

Here are (1) *some* tips to help you get on well with (2) ___________ French on your next visit to (3) ___________ beautiful country. When you first meet someone, do not start using (4) ___________ first name, except with (5) ___________ younger people. It is best to wait to be invited to use (6) ___________ first names. The proper way to greet someone is 'Bonjour, Monsieur or Madame.' (7) ___________ French like conversation. When you are speaking to (8) ___________ French people, do not be surprised if they keep interrupting you and even raise (9) ___________ voices; it is quite normal. (10) ___________ French people shake hands much more than (11) ___________ Americans or most Europeans: if you fail to shake (12) ___________ hands, you may be considered rude. Close friends will kiss (13) ___________ cheeks (once, twice, even three times). However, it is more a light touching of cheeks than (14) ___________ true kiss. One of (15) ___________ most common mistakes non-native speakers of (16) ___________ French make is when expressing their age. In many languages one says 'I am X years old', whereas in French one says, 'I have X years.'

Word order

6 Put these statements about customs and culture into the correct order.

1 should/talk/you/at/small/parties/make (Britain)
You should make small talk at parties.

2 on/for/should/meetings/be/always/you/time (Britain)
____

3 must/people/too/not/you/stand/to/close (Britain)
____

4 the/eight/number/luckiest/is (China)
____

5 never/the/jump/must/you/queue (Britain)
____

6 avoid/'no'/directly/they/saying (Japan)
____

7 they/use/titles/'Herr'/often/'Mr'/formal/for/like (Germany)
____

8 other/often/each/they/interrupt (France)
____

9 women/kiss/friends/especially/close/may/cheeks (France)
____

10 add/family/mother's/theirs/adults/to/their/name (Latin America)
____

7 Are the statements in exercise 6 true for your country? Write similar sentences about customs and culture in your country, using the topics in brackets.

1 (parties) ______________________________
____

2 (business) ______________________________
____

3 (lucky numbers or objects) ______________________________
____

4 (politeness) ______________________________
____

5 (meeting new people) ______________________________
____

VOCABULARY

1 Most of the words below can be both verbs and nouns. Underline the ones that are only verbs and circle the ones that are only nouns.

park visit food drink meet talk shop buy eat dress stroll lamp turn suit order pay

Now complete these sentences using one of the words above in each space.

1 After the meal, how about going to the pub for a ____________ ?
2 You got that CD for only five pounds? That was a very good ____________ !
3 Whose ____________ is it to answer the next question?
4 I always ____________ at the supermarket – it's quicker and cheaper.
5 There's nothing like a ____________ along the sea front on a sunny Sunday morning.
6 'When I give an ____________ , I expect you to obey,' said the general.
7 Why don't we pay our neighbours a ____________ on Christmas Eve?

Word formation

2 Complete this table.

verb	noun	verb	noun
advertise		disappear	
appoint		inform	
arrange		introduce	
arrive		know	
assist		persuade	
direct		refresh	

Phrasal verbs with *turn*

3 Match the words and phrases below with the phrasal verbs they go with. Many of the words and phrases go with more than one phrasal verb.

the tap	a proposal	the radio	to be true	the central heating
at the frontier	the light	crime	a suggestion	to be someone else
the TV	at a party	drugs	an application	because the road was blocked
an offer	the volume			

1 turn back ____________________

____

2 turn down ____________________

____

3 turn off ____________________

____

4 turn on ____________________

____

5 turn out ____________________

____

6 turn to ____________________

____

7 turn up ____________________

____

5 Comic genius

GRAMMAR AND USE OF ENGLISH

Exam practice: Use of English, Part 1

1 For questions 1–15, read the text below and decide which answer A, B, C or D best fits each space.

Laurel or Hardy?

He was a music-hall comedian in England before he went to America in 1910. In those (0) ___C___ he often (1) ________ Chaplin. He made his first short film in 1918 but did not (2) ________ to establish himself in the competitive (3) ________ of screen comedy. The first film he made with his famous fat (4) ________ was called *Putting Pants on Philip* in 1927. Many critics (5) ________ that he was the more creative (6) ________ of the partnership. The humorist Leo McCarey (7) ________ him a rare comic who was intelligent (8) ________ to make up his own gags. (9) ________ , he was remarkably talented, while his partner was (10) ________ so and this is the key to understanding their relationship. As a (11) ________ , throughout their career together he (12) ________ on being paid twice as much as his friend because he believed he was (13) ________ twice as much. While he wrote the films and (14) ________ part in their creation, his partner was incapable of creating anything at all – it was amazing how he managed to find his (15) ________ to the studio.

0	A times	B periods	C days	D weeks
1	A copied	B followed	C resembled	D liked
2	A succeed	B reach	C fail	D manage
3	A job	B field	C position	D place
4	A pair	B colleague	C partner	D match
5	A persist	B claim	C refuse	D review
6	A person	B member	C actor	D piece
7	A considered	B said	C described	D saw
8	A even	B quite	C enough	D also
9	A Although	B Moreover	C However	D So
10	A less	B least	C little	D hardly
11	A fact	B conclusion	C matter	D result
12	A persisted	B insisted	C kept	D demanded
13	A valued	B making	C worth	D acting
14	A took	B made	C was	D had
15	A car	B road	C route	D way

Which of the two famous comedians, Laurel or Hardy, does the text describe?

Exam practice: Use of English, Part 4

2 For questions 1–15, read the text below and look carefully at each line. Some of the lines are correct, and some have a word which should not be there. If a line is correct, put a tick (✓). If a line has a word which should not be there, write the word.

A sense of humour

___✓___ 0 Have you noticed how often people are happy to hear the same joke,
___*not*___ 00 over and over again? One reason, of course, is that they have not
________ 1 probably forgotten the details of the joke, but I am sure it also has
________ 2 something to do with getting at the same pleasure more than once. So
________ 3 when a person who has just started telling a joke asks his audience,
________ 4 'Do you know it?' or 'Have you heard it before?' people must always
________ 5 answer something like, 'It doesn't matter, let's hear it again.' It is not such
________ 6 surprising that if a joke is worth hearing, it is worth hearing several times.
________ 7 I think it was Ogden Nash who once said that it is probably better to have
________ 8 an infectious disease than to have a sense of humour. He argued,
________ 9 tongue-in-cheek no doubt, that although that people who possess a sense
________ 10 of humour have a good time, they do never actually achieve anything
________ 11 important, whether good or bad. This, thought Nash, is because when
________ 12 people with a sense of the humour begin to do anything important, they
________ 13 can't help noticing how so funny they look doing it, so they stop to have
________ 14 a good laugh at themselves. As a result, what might to have been a
________ 15 great achievement is left unfinished.

Exam practice: Use of English, Part 5

3 For questions 1–10, read the jokes below. Use the word given in capitals at the end of each line to form a word that fits in the space in the same line.

1 The boss of a big company brought all his (0) ___*employees*___ together — EMPLOY
and told them he had an (1) ________________ to make. He told them he had — ANNOUNCE
some good news and some bad news for them. 'It is my (2) ________________ — PLEASE
to announce,' he said, 'that we have kept to all (3) ________________ — GOVERN
regulations and we haven't broken any laws.' Everyone smiled with
(4) ________________ . 'The bad news,' he continued, 'is that ... — SATISFY

2 What are the (5) ________________ for any young person who wishes to — QUALIFY
become a (6) ________________ ? He should be able to foretell what is going — POLITICS
to happen tomorrow, next week, next month and next year and have the
(7) ________________ afterwards to explain why ... — ABLE

3 A judge, in sentencing a (8) ________________ recently, said: 'I'm going to give — CRIME
you the maximum (9) ________________ . I'm going to let you go free, so you — PUNISH
can worry about taxes, inflation, (10) ________________ bills and everything else, ... — ELECTRIC

Now match the jokes with these punchlines. There is one extra punchline which you do not need to use.

... just like the rest of us. ... they never do. ... we are bankrupt. ... it didn't happen.

Past simple and past continuous

Exam practice: Use of English, Part 3

4 For questions 1–10, complete the second sentence so that it has a similar meaning to the first sentence, using the word given. Do not change the word given. You must use between two and five words, including the word given.

0 My sister is not old enough to ride a bicycle.
too
My sister is ___too young to___ ride a bicycle.

1 During his law studies he met his future wife.
studying
While ______________________ he met his future wife.

2 She had more freedom when her father was abroad.
travelling
While ______________________ she had more freedom.

3 I had been at the party too long and I was bored.
enjoying
I ______________________ because I had been there too long.

4 Andrew said the mistake was my fault.
blamed
Andrew ______________________ the mistake.

5 He misbehaved all the time, even when the teacher told him off.
always
He ______________________ , even when the teacher told him off.

6 He was an actor in a lot of plays at school.
acting
He did ______________________ at school.

7 It was raining all evening.
stop
It ______________________ all evening.

8 It was windy all day yesterday.
blowing
A ______________________ all day yesterday.

9 When he got to the party everyone was chatting and eating.
arrival
On ______________________ the party everyone was chatting and eating.

10 They ate dinner and discussed the problem at the same time.
were
While ______________________ discussed the problem.

5 Match the clauses in list A with the clauses in list B to make complete sentences.

A	B
1 He stayed up late	a because he was trying to lose weight.
2 He had his hair cut	b because she was wearing jeans.
3 She looked much younger	c because the baby was crying.
4 She laughed	d because he was leaving.
5 I wish I had worn my overcoat	e because it was freezing outside.
6 He packed his bags	f because music was playing in the background.
7 He refused to eat any cake	g because he was going into the army.
8 He felt very uncomfortable	h because he was revising for an exam.
9 I couldn't hear a word she said	i because he was sitting on the floor.
10 The atmosphere was pleasant	j because people were telling jokes.

6 Complete these sentences using the past continuous form of one of the verbs below in each space. Use one of the verbs twice.

sleep have go wear do rain feel watch prepare

1 I went to bed early because I ___*was feeling*___ tired.
2 At the funeral everyone ______________ black.
3 He learnt the text by heart when he ______________ for the exam.
4 He couldn't answer the phone because he ______________ a bath.
5 She lost her purse while she ______________ the shopping.
6 When he got home at three in the morning everyone ______________ .
7 They couldn't go for a picnic because it ______________ outside.
8 He can't be the murderer because he ______________ TV all evening.
9 I didn't recognize her because she ______________ an unusual costume.
10 The telephone rang just as I ______________ to bed.

7 Answer these questions using the past simple or the past continuous. You can use some of the verbs below.

dance	**jump**	**watch**	**scream**	**celebrate**	**laugh**
answer	**sleep**	**sit**	**read**	**shout**	**misbehave**

1 a What did you do when the telephone rang?

____

b What were you doing when the telephone rang?

____

2 a What did the pupils do when the teacher came in?

____

b What were the pupils doing when the teacher came in?

____

3 a What was everyone at the party doing when the lights went out?

____

b What did everyone at the party do when the lights went out?

____

4 a What were you doing when the fire broke out?

____

b What did you do when the fire broke out?

____

5 a What were you doing when you heard about your success in the exam?

____

b What did you do when you heard about your success in the exam?

____

VOCABULARY

Word formation

1 Make nouns from the words in the box by adding the appropriate suffix: *-ship*, *-ment* or *-ness*.

member	appoint	champion	empty	enjoy	good	excite	fond	friend	entertain
happy	hard	lazy	manage	amuse	partner	retire	sad	scholar	stingy

-ship	*-ment*	*-ness*
championship	_______	_______
_______	_______	_______
_______	_______	_______
_______	_______	_______
_______	_______	_______
_______	_______	_______
_______	_______	_______

2 Complete these sentences using one of the words from exercise 1 in each space.

1 Scrooge is famous for his _______________ with money.
2 Money doesn't always bring _______________ ; rich people are often miserable.
3 How much does _______________ of that club cost?
4 I can't see you at five because I have another _______________ .
5 A good adventure film is usually full of _______________ .
6 He went into _______________ with his best friend but the business went bankrupt.
7 My favourite form of _______________ is the cinema.
8 Which team do you think is going to win the _______________ ?

Theatre

3 Match the words in list A with their meanings in list B.

1 playwright	a when the audience clap their hands to show they like something
2 set	b the place where the actors walk and talk
3 role	c the part an actor plays
4 box office	d the person who writes the text for the actors
5 applause	e where the action takes place, for example in a room or a forest
6 scene	f what we can see in the background, often painted
7 director	g where they sell tickets
8 stage	h the person who tells the actors what to do

4 Now write definitions for these words.

9 actor ____________________

10 comedy ____________________

11 scenery ____________________

12 critic ____________________

13 character ____________________

14 comedian ____________________

Phrasal verbs with *take*

5 Replace the underlined words in these sentences with the correct form of one of the phrasal verbs below. Make any other changes that are necessary. Use one of the phrasal verbs twice.

take in **take after** **take up** **take off** **take to** **take down** **take back**

1 He is just like his grandfather.
He takes after his grandfather.

2 I'm afraid I didn't like John at first; it took me some time to like him.

____

3 If I were you, I would return it to the shop and ask for a refund.

____

4 I didn't realize what he was saying because my mind was on something else.

____

5 Why don't you accept the offer of a job with the record company?

____

6 If you pay cash, I'll give it to you for five pounds less.

____

7 I made a note of the most important points in his lecture.

____

8 I was deceived by his lies.

____

6 Talking sense

GRAMMAR AND USE OF ENGLISH

Exam practice: Use of English, Part 2

1 For questions 1–15, read the text below and think of the word which best fits each space. Use only one word in each space.

How do we see in 3D?

When we look across a field, how (0) ___*do*___ we know that one distant object is bigger than another (1) __________ that one object is behind another, not in (2) __________ of it? In (3) __________ words, how do we see things in three dimensions, in proper relation to (4) __________ other, instead of seeing everything 'flat'? The answer is that (5) __________ we see things, we see them not (6) __________ with our eyes but with (7) __________ minds as well: we see things (8) __________ the light of experience. Our minds and memories help (9) __________ to interpret what we see. For instance, experience gives us an idea about the size (10) __________ things. A man (11) __________ a boat some distance from the shore looks much smaller (12) __________ a man on the beach. But you don't think (13) __________ one is a very large man and the (14) __________ a very small man. What you say to yourself is that one man is nearby and the other is (15) __________ away.

Exam practice: Use of English, Part 4

2 For questions 1–15, read the text below and look carefully at each line. Some of the lines are correct, and some have a word which should not be there. If a line is correct, put a tick (✓). If a line has a word which should not be there, write the word.

How do bats know where they are going?

___*a*___ 0 An odd thing about bats is that they do not have a good
___✓___ 00 eyesight, although they have to hunt for their food during
________ 1 the night. In fact, bats do not rely on their eyes to find out
________ 2 their way. They use a kind of radar system which works
________ 3 like this: when they fly, bats make high-pitched sounds
________ 4 which are so high that human beings cannot yet hear
________ 5 them. The echoes from these sounds are thrown back to
________ 6 the bat while it is still in to the air. The bat can tell whether
________ 7 the echo came from an object nearby or much far away
________ 8 and it will change the direction of its flight to avoid to
________ 9 crashing into the object. Bats depend on flying more than
________ 10 most animals. While birds and insects also fly, they have
________ 11 and the ability to walk about if necessary. However, a
________ 12 bat cannot walk very easily because of its limbs and
________ 13 feet are not suitable; it cannot even stand very easily.
________ 14 So it is actually then easier for a bat to hang upside
________ 15 down from a branch than to sit on it.

Exam practice: Use of English, Part 5

3 For questions 1–10, read the text below. Use the word given in capitals at the end of each line to form a word that fits in the space in the same line.

All about owls

For thousands of years the owl has been a (0) *creature* which	CREATE
has had a special (1) ________________ for people. Primitive people had	MEAN
many superstitions about the owl, (2) ________________ because of the	MAIN
strange sound of the cries it makes. In many parts of Europe, the	
hooting of an owl is (3) ________________ to be an omen of death.	THINK
In ancient Greece, the owl was a symbol of (4) ________________ so it	WISE
was closely linked with the female (5) ________________ Athena.	GOD
The owl is a bird that really comes to life at night and its whole	
body is (6) ________________ suited to this way of living.	SPECIAL
An owl has very (7) ________________ hearing and a remarkable	SENSE
(8) ________________ to see in the dark. If there are any other animals	ABLE
around at night, it will hear them (9) ________________ , and because the	IMMEDIATE
owl is so (10) ________________ of its territory, it will frighten them away	PROTECT
with its strange hoot.	

Comparative and superlative adjectives

Exam practice: Use of English, Part 3

4 For questions 1–10, complete the second sentence so that it has a similar meaning to the first sentence, using the word given. Do not change the word given. You must use between two and five words, including the word given.

0 My sister is not old enough to ride a bicycle.
too
My sister is ________ *too young to* ________ ride a bicycle.

1 Objects that are close are clearer than objects that are distant.
clear
Distant objects ________________________________ close objects.

2 This month's test and last month's test were equally easy.
just
This month's test ________________________________ last month's test.

3 My brother lives nearer to me than my mother does.
far
My brother does not ________________________________ from me as my mother does.

4 As people get older their eyesight becomes weaker.
worse
The ______________________________ your eyesight becomes.

5 Birds have better eyesight than we have.
good
Our eyesight ______________________________ that of birds.

6 The elephant is the heaviest animal in the world.
heavier
No animal in the world ______________________________ an elephant.

7 In many countries people choose a dog as a pet.
popular
Dogs ______________________________ in many countries.

8 Our sense of smell is not as good as that of most animals.
have
Most animals ______________________________ sense of smell than us.

9 There's no animal as beautiful as a horse.
most
Horses are ______________________________ of all.

10 Cats are not as loyal as dogs.
more
Dogs ______________________________ cats.

5 Choose the correct word or words in these sentences, then decide whether the sentences are true or false.

How much do you know about elephants?	**True/False**
1 The elephant has the longer/longest nose (or trunk) in the animal kingdom.	________
2 The elephant does much/more with its nose than/that any other animal.	________
3 There are most/more than/of 40 000 muscles in an elephant's trunk.	________
4 Elephants have worse/worser memories than most animals.	________
5 An elephant can run more fast/faster than a human being.	________
6 The mammoth was as big/no bigger than the present day elephant.	________
7 Elephants are the largest/most large land animals.	________
8 Elephants can be trained more easily/easier than any other animal.	________
9 The Asian elephant's ears are just as bigger/big as/than the African elephant's.	________
10 An elephant eats as more/much as 225 kilos a day.	________

(See page 35 for the answers to the quiz.)

VOCABULARY

Word formation

1 Complete this table.

verb	noun	noun (person)
act		(man) (woman)
appear		
detect		
direct		
discover		
entertain		
examine		
explode		
follow		
immigrate		
inhabit		
manage		
protect		
speak		
understand		

How many suffixes are there for different kinds of people in the table?

2 Match the words for people from the table above with these definitions.

1 a person who goes to other countries to find work = ________________
2 a person who checks your answers and gives you marks = ________________
3 a person who lives in a place = ________________
4 a person who finds things and people = ________________
5 a person who finds countries = ________________
6 a person who is in charge = ________________ /________________ (two words)
7 a person who keeps you from harm = ________________
8 a person who is a supporter or fan of someone else = ________________
9 a person who talks in public = ________________
10 a person who performs on stage = ________________ /________________ /________________ (three words)

Animals

3 Use the clues to complete the names of these animals.

1 the biggest land animal = e _ _ _ _ _ _ t
2 the fastest dog = g _ _ _ h _ _ _ d
3 the tallest animal = g _ _ _ _ _ e
4 one of the most useful animals to people = h _ _ _ e
5 one of the biggest and most powerful birds = e _ _ _ e
6 one of the heaviest animals = h _ _ _ _ _ _ _ _ _ _ s
7 one of the longest and most poisonous animals = s _ _ _ e
8 one of the biggest birds but the worst at flying = o _ _ _ _ _ h
9 one of the most dangerous insects = m _ _ _ _ _ _ o
10 one of the most poisonous creatures = s _ _ _ _ _ _ n
11 the fastest animal in the world = c _ _ _ _ _ h
12 the biggest creature of all = w _ _ _ e
13 the most dangerous creature in the sea = s _ _ _ k
14 one of the smallest and most common insects = a _ _
15 the most talkative bird = p _ _ _ _ t
16 one of the slowest animals = t _ _ _ _ _ _ e

Phrasal verbs with *go*

4 Complete these sentences using the correct form of one of the phrasal verbs below in each space. Use each phrasal verb more than once.

go out   go off   go through   go down   go on   go up

1 I'm *going through* a hard time at the moment.
2 I can't ______________________ – I've had enough!
3 I set the alarm to ______________________ at seven o'clock.
4 Who's Mary ______________________ with nowadays?
5 The show ______________________ very well with audiences.
6 There was a fire and the building ______________________ in smoke.
7 I'm ______________________ to the north of the country to visit friends.
8 She just ______________________ without saying anything.
9 The temperature's ______________________ today; it's colder.
10 What was ______________________ your mind before the operation?
11 She ______________________ of the building and through the main gate.
12 Don't keep ______________________ about your ex-boyfriend; it's boring.
13 Prices are always ______________________ , aren't they?
14 This cheese has ______________________ . Throw it away.
15 Let's ______________________ these figures. We must make sure they are accurate.
16 Please ______________________ and finish your story.

Answers for the elephant quiz, page 33

1 True.
2 True. An elephant does all of the following with its trunk: smells; breathes; sprays water (or sand) over its body; puts its food in its mouth; blows trumpet calls; pulls down trees; detects insects in the air and carries heavy objects.
3 True.
4 False. They have good memories; if you attack them, they won't forget it!
5 False. The world record for a human runner is 43.37 km per hour. The top speed of an elephant is 40 km per hour.
6 True. It was about the size of an African elephant.
7 True.
8 False. Dolphins and primates are easier to train.
9 False. They are smaller.
10 True.

7 Leisure for pleasure

GRAMMAR AND USE OF ENGLISH

Exam practice: Use of English, Part 1

1 For questions 1–15, read the text below and decide which answer A, B, C or D best fits each space.

A visit to Toledo

Toledo (0) ___B___ out dramatically against the blue, Castillian sky. It is as spectacular (1) ________ it is rich in history. Every corner of the city has a tale to be (2) ________ which reflects a brilliant (3) ________ in Spanish history. There is something to see and enjoy at every (4) ________ in Toledo. Walking along the maze of narrow, winding lanes you (5) ________ churches, old houses and palaces. Allow at (6) ________ one whole day for your visit as there are many (7) ________ which should not be (8) ________ . The magnificent Cathedral, which dates back to the thirteenth century, is of (9) ________ interest. Another unique experience is the El Greco House and Museum. In 1585, El Greco (10) ________ into a house which must have been (11) ________ to this attractive, sixteenth century Toledan house. On the first (12) ________ of the museum is a complete series of individual portraits of the Apostles, a later series (13) ________ the one in the Cathedral. In the Church of Santo Tomé you will find one of El Greco's finest (14) ________ , 'The Burial of Count Orgaz'. Remember also to (15) ________ a visit to the Alcázar, which stands massive and proud as ever, dominating all other buildings.

	A	B	C	D
0	A goes	B stands	C puts	D brings
1	A like	B how	C than	D as
2	A said	B listened	C told	D counted
3	A year	B view	C part	D period
4	A place	B step	C point	D area
5	A pass	B cross	C spot	D glance
6	A last	B most	C once	D least
7	A scenes	B sights	C views	D sides
8	A lost	B wasted	C forgotten	D missed
9	A little	B enough	C outstanding	D excellent
10	A rented	B entered	C changed	D moved
11	A similar	B same	C like	D resembled
12	A stage	B space	C floor	D ground
13	A than	B that	C of	D with
14	A tasks	B jobs	C masters	D works
15	A give	B pay	C do	D pass

Exam practice: Use of English, Part 4

2 For questions 1–15, read the text below and look carefully at each line. Some of the lines are correct, and some have a word which should not be there. If a line is correct, put a tick (✓). If a line has a word which should not be there, write the word.

Strasbourg

✓ 0 Strasbourg has always been an important European city.
✓ 00 Thanks to a favourable geographical position – at the
________ 1 crossroads of waterways and overland routes – the area
________ 2 on which the Strasbourg now stands has been inhabited
________ 3 for since the Bronze Age. In the Middle Ages, it was an
________ 4 important economic centre and it has gradually grew so
________ 5 strong that by the fifteenth century it had become a free
________ 6 republic. It grew more richer and richer in the sixteenth
________ 7 century and welcomed free thinkers and refugees from
________ 8 Switzerland, Italy and France. These newcomers have
________ 9 greatly enriched the city's cultural life. In 1697, Strasbourg
________ 10 has became part of France. Germany conquered it in 1870
________ 11 and it was only returned to France after the end of the First
________ 12 World War. It was again occupied by Germany in the Second
________ 13 World War and suffered some great destruction. In 1949, the
________ 14 city was been chosen to be the headquarters of the Council
________ 15 of Europe, and since 1979 it has been come the seat of the
European Parliament to which, at present, fifteen countries
send representatives.

Exam practice: Use of English, Part 5

3 For questions 1–10, read the text below. Use the word given in capitals at the end of each line to form a word that fits in the space in the same line.

Madame Tussaud's

Madame Tussaud's is one of the most popular (0) *attractions* in	ATTRACT
London and as it is very (1) ________ in summer, make sure	CROWD
you get there early. This famous and highly (2) ________	ENTERTAIN
museum contains life-like wax figures, which are (3) ________	CONTINUE
brought up to date. On display are (4) ________ models of	REAL
famous people, from the latest pop stars to (5) ________ figures.	HISTORY
You can also see today's politicians and the most well-known TV	
(6) ________ . You can buy a combined ticket which will allow	PERSON
you (7) ________ to both the Museum and the Planetarium next	ADMIT
door. The Planetarium is open (8) ________ from 10.00 am to	DAY
5.30 pm and (9) ________ are given every hour. Baker Street is	PRESENT
the (10) ________ underground station for both attractions.	NEAR

Present perfect simple and present perfect continuous

Exam practice: Use of English, Part 3

4 For questions 1–10, complete the second sentence so that it has a similar meaning to the first sentence, using the word given. Do not change the word given. You must use between two and five words, including the word given.

0 My sister is not old enough to ride a bicycle.
too
My sister is ______ *too young to* ______ ride a bicycle.

1 The building was first used in the nineteenth century.
since
The building ______________________ the nineteenth century.

2 This is not my first visit to Toledo.
been
I ______________________ before.

3 Maria started learning to drive last year.
learning
Maria ______________________ since last year.

4 There are far more theatres in the city than there used to be.
built
A lot ______________________ in the city recently.

5 I started correcting these tests yesterday and I still haven't finished.
been
I ______________________ since yesterday.

6 The exhibition opened just a few days ago.
only
The exhibition ______________________ opened.

7 Films on TV are better now than when I was a child.
improved
Films on TV ______________________ I was a child.

8 I moved here a couple of months ago.
living
I ______________________ two months.

9 I first started learning Spanish when I went to Mexico for a holiday.
since
I ______________________ I went to Mexico for a holiday.

10 It's five years since we went to Ireland.
for
We have ______________________ five years.

5 Choose the correct tense in these sentences.

1 The grocer's shop has been closing/has closed since the supermarket opened.
2 He has made/He made several films already.
3 Millions of people have been seeing/have seen the film on TV.
4 I've been reading/I've read a marvellous novel. I can't wait to find out what happens.
5 I went/I have been going to school when I was five.
6 We've sold/We've been selling the last copies of the book – sorry.
7 I've written/I've been writing a postcard to John, now I am writing one to Peter.
8 You look as if you've cried/you've been crying.
9 Come in, the party's not over yet and we've had/we've been having a great time. Do you want a drink?
10 I've been thinking/I've thought ... Wouldn't it be nice if we had a new car?

VOCABULARY

Word formation

1 Make adjectives by combining the words below with the affixes *in-*, *pre-*, *-al* and *-ful*.

famous historic classic complete colour direct wonder music nation care view

in-	*pre-*	*-al*	*-ful*
infamous			

2 Complete these sentences using one of the words from exercise 1 in each space.

1 I am not very __________________ . I can't play any instrument, I'm afraid.
2 Your test was __________________ ; you only did four out of five questions.
3 Dinosaurs and other __________________ creatures disappeared during the Ice Age.
4 Your room is very __________________ with all these reds and greens.
5 Do you know the words of your __________________ anthem?
6 Al Capone was a/an __________________ gangster.
7 The castle is a/an __________________ building so they can't knock it down.

3 Complete this table.

verb	noun	adjective
		dedicated
		punishable
reside		
		dominant
repute		reputable
		impressive
		exploratory
	interest	1 2
exhaust		1 2
entertain		1 2

4 Complete these sentences using one of the words from the table above in each space.

1 I am absolutely ________________ ! I must lie down and rest.
2 They went on a journey of ________________ into Africa.
3 You made a very good ________________ at the interview.
4 He has an excellent ________________ as a lawyer, so you're bound to win the case.
5 The castle at the top of the hill ________________ the whole landscape.
6 Our house is in a quiet ________________ area of the city.
7 The criminal escaped ________________ because there was little concrete evidence.

Collective nouns

5 Complete these sentences with an appropriate auxiliary verb or a pronoun.

1 The government ___*has*___ said it will raise taxes.
2 The government have made up _________ mind to increase pensions.
3 The public _________ deceived by the lie the politicians told them.
4 The public wants a government which _________ can trust.
5 The family next door _________ selling its old furniture.
6 My family are proud of _________ past.
7 The jury is considering _________ decision.
8 The jury _________ decided on their verdict.
9 The team _________ won all their matches this season.
10 The team _________ not won a single one of its matches this season.

Phrasal verbs

6 Match the phrasal verbs in list A with their meanings in list B.

A	B
1 catch on	a escape
2 get away	b consider
3 go on	c check (information)
4 let down	d continue
5 look on	e pretend
6 look up	f disappoint
7 put on	g become popular

7 Match the sentences in list A with the appropriate responses in list B.

A	B
1 Can I trust you with all this responsibility?	a Rubbish! He's putting it on.
2 Why have you stopped? We haven't got to the top yet.	b Why don't you look it up?
3 I wish I knew what 'serendipity' meant.	c It looks weird; it'll never catch on.
4 The place is surrounded by the police.	d I promise I won't let you down.
5 The centre forward is on the ground and is in great pain.	e They'll never get away.
6 Why are you asking me to do this?	f I can't go on – I'm exhausted.
7 Look at my new hair style, isn't it great?	g I look on you as a real friend, someone I can rely on.

8 Sherlock Holmes – The Mystery of the Creeping Man

GRAMMAR AND USE OF ENGLISH

Exam practice: Use of English, Part 2

1 For questions 1–15, read the text below and think of the word which best fits each space. Use only one word in each space.

Holmes rides again

I had (0) ___not___ seen Holmes for some time and had no idea what he had been doing since the last time we (1) ___________ worked together on the Case of the Creeping Man. He was in a chatty mood (2) ___________ morning and settled me into the low arm-chair on (3) ___________ side of the fire, while he sat (4) ___________ in the opposite chair, puffing away at his pipe as usual.

Suddenly, the door flew open and a huge man burst (5) ___________ the room. It (6) ___________ have been funny if he hadn't looked (7) ___________ frightening, with his sullen, dark eyes with a gleam of malice in them and his muscular figure. The man immediately asked which (8) ___________ us was Master Holmes. The famous detective raised (9) ___________ pipe with a smile. 'Oh, it's you, is it?' said our visitor. 'Well, you keep your nose (10) ___________ of other people's business.' Holmes asked the stranger to go (11) ___________ . 'I've handled your sort before now,' the man continued, 'so just watch (12) ___________ .' He swung his huge fist under my friend's nose. Holmes examined (13) ___________ closely with an air of great interest. It may have (14) ___________ my friend's cool response (15) ___________ my picking up the poker, but our visitor then calmed down a little.

Exam practice: Use of English, Part 4

2 For questions 1–15, read the text below and look carefully at each line. Some of the lines are correct, and some have a word which should not be there. If a line is correct, put a tick (✓). If a line has a word which should not be there, write the word.

A close look

___just___ 0 Sherlock Holmes had just been bending over a microscope for a long
___has___ 00 time. Now he has straightened himself and looked at me in triumph.
________ 1 He informed me that the objects he had been examining had glue on
________ 2 them. 'There's no doubt about it,' he said. I was looked through the
________ 3 microscope and agreed that, apart from some of hairs and dust, there
________ 4 were traces of glue clearly visible. We had been found the objects
________ 5 scattered in a field near the body of the dead policeman. A cap
________ 6 which belonging to the accused was also found at the crime scene,
________ 7 but he had denied that it was his. The accused was a picture framer
________ 8 who habitually handled glue. The case Holmes was investigating
________ 9 in was not one of his own; Inspector Merivale of Scotland Yard

________ 10 had asked my friend to look into the murder. In so doing, Holmes had had
________ 11 discovered the importance of the microscope in the work of a detective.
________ 12 Holmes then told me he was expecting a new client to arrive but that
________ 13 the man was so late. Suddenly he asked me if I knew anything about
________ 14 racing. I admitted I occasionally was spent some of my war pension on
________ 15 betting on the horses but I rarely won anything. 'Then I'll need your advice,' said Holmes.

Exam practice: Use of English, Part 5

3 For questions 1–10, read the text below. Use the word given in capitals at the end of each line to form a word that fits in the space in the same line.

Unsolved mysteries

I have a (0) ___briefcase___ full of papers which describe cases	BRIEF
Sherlock Holmes has investigated. Some are (1) ________________ ,	FAIL
since there were no final (2) ________________ for the mysteries in	EXPLAIN
question. A problem without a (3) ________________ may interest the	SOLVE
(4) ________________ , but will offer little to the general reader.	SPECIAL
Among these (5) ________________ stories is that of the yacht *Alicia*,	FINISH
which one morning sailed into the mist and (6) ________________ forever;	APPEAR
the vessel and the crew were never seen again. Then there was	
the case of the well-known (7) ________________ Luigi Persano, who	JOURNAL
was found (8) ________________ mad with a jar in front of him. The jar	COMPLETE
contained a remarkable worm, unknown to science up to that point.	
Apart from these mysterious cases for which Holmes did not find	
solutions, there are those which various (9) ________________ people	INFLUENCE
would rather not see in print and those which might affect the	
(10) ________________ of Holmes himself, for whom I have more respect	REPUTE
than for any man alive.	

Past perfect simple and past perfect continuous

Exam practice: Use of English, Part 3

4 For questions 1–10, complete the second sentence so that it has a similar meaning to the first sentence, using the word given. Do not change the word given. You must use between two and five words, including the word given.

0 My sister is not old enough to ride a bicycle.
too
My sister is ___too young to___ ride a bicycle.

1 First he entered the house through the window and then he stole the jewels.
broken
After ________________________________ the house through the window he stole the jewels.

2 His first bank robbery was two years ago.
robbed
He ______________________________ two years before.

3 After walking five miles he was tired.
come
He ______________________________ foot and was tired.

4 I came back home after living in Australia for ten years.
been
I ______________________________ Australia for ten years when I came back home.

5 His success in business allowed him to retire early.
had
He retired early ______________________________ in business.

6 As soon as she came into the room she announced her marriage.
got
She told us ______________________________ as soon as she came into the room.

7 Claire locked the door after turning off all the lights.
turned
After ______________________________ all the lights she locked the door.

8 There was no one in the room when the police arrived.
left
Everyone ______________________________ the time the police arrived.

9 His acting in a play caused him to lose his voice.
performing
He lost his voice because ______________________________ in a play.

10 She was exhausted after driving all night.
been
She ______________________________ all night so she was exhausted.

5 Match the questions in list A with their answers in list B.

A	B
1 Why was there a water shortage that summer?	a He had given up smoking.
2 How did she manage to lose so much weight?	b He had spotted mud in her shoes.
3 Why did the teacher ask him to leave the room?	c She had been on a diet for months.
4 Why was he feeling much healthier?	d He had been misbehaving all morning.
5 Why did the police stop him?	e He had been behaving very strangely.
6 Why did she think he had been taking drugs?	f It hadn't rained for a long time.
7 How did the detective know she had been out in the rain?	g He had been driving while drunk.

6 Complete the answers in list B with the correct form (past perfect simple or continuous) of the verbs in brackets, then match the answers with the questions in list A.

A	B
1 Why were you depressed?	a Someone ___had tipped___ (tip) them off.
2 Why was he late for the exam?	b He ________ (come) up with a new theory.
3 How did the police know where the drugs were?	c She ________ (live) in Paris as a child.
4 Why were the flowers dead?	d I ________ (fail) my exam.
5 Why was Colombus tired?	e He ________ (study) all night.
6 Why was Einstein happy?	f He ________ (travel) a long time.
7 Why did she speak with a French accent?	g Because he ______ (already/see) it.
8 Why didn't he want to go and see the film?	h We ________ (forget) to water them.

VOCABULARY

Phrasal verbs and idioms with *back*

1 Replace the underlined words in these sentences with the correct form of one of the phrasal verbs below. Make any other changes that are necessary.

look back **keep back** **give back** **cut back on** **call back** **bring back** **take back**

1 I'll lend you my book if you promise to return it.

____

2 He asked his old girlfriend to go out with him again, but she refused to accept him again.

____

3 When I phoned she was busy and she still hasn't returned my call.

____

4 Don't think about the past, think about the future.

____

5 Excuse me, I'm returning this plate because it is cracked.

____

6 If you withhold important evidence from the police, you could get into trouble.

____

7 We'll have to reduce our expenses. We can't afford to spend so much.

____

Word formation

2 Complete this table.

verb	adjective	noun
		curiosity
		fury
inform		
	exaggerated	
interrupt		
	celebratory	
object	objectionable	
suggest		
arrive		
	approving	
		gloom
think	1 2 thoughtless	
	understandable	
		activity
		danger
		mystery
excite	1 2	
terrify	1 2	

3 Complete these sentences using one of the words from the table above in each space.

1 What a dark room – it's so ________________ in here!
2 Sherlock Holmes was called in to solve the ________________ .
3 My parents don't ________________ of my friends because they don't have regular jobs.
4 My parents ________________ to my staying out late if they don't know where I am.
5 How are we going to ________________ our victory in the competition?
6 Climbing up that steep mountain looks ________________ to me because I'm scared of heights.
7 He led an ________________ life till he was in his 80s and even carried on working till he died.
8 It was very ________________ of you to visit me in hospital – I'm very grateful.
9 If the pupils don't ________________ the explanation, I repeat it using simpler words.
10 The programme was ________________ to bring viewers an important newsflash.

9 Mysterious monsters

GRAMMAR AND USE OF ENGLISH

Exam practice: Use of English, Part 1

1 For questions 1–15, read the text below and decide which answer A, B, C or D best fits each space.

The monster in the lake

A 34-year-old librarian from Clifden in County Galway claims she and a friend (0) __C__ a large serpent-like monster in Lake Fadda in western Ireland on Wednesday afternoon as they were picnicking near the (1) ________ of the lake. Local police are (2) ________ the story, which follows a series of similar reports in (3) ________ years. Researchers at Trinity College, Dublin have also (4) ________ an interest in the reports. Georgia Cranberry, the wife of a local businessman, (5) ________ what she and her friend saw at about three o'clock last Wednesday as 'a huge monster writhing in the water (6) ________ a snake, about 30 metres (7) ________ '. Her friend, Mary Reilly, a shop assistant in a department store in Galway, (8) ________ the story and added: 'We were (9) ________ . The creature was enormous and it swam with its mouth open. It was (10) ________ like those pictures of the Loch Ness Monster.' More (11) ________ were not available as before they were (12) ________ to take a photograph of the monster it disappeared below the (13) ________ of the lake, which is nearly half a mile long. The description given to police by the two women (14) ________ that of other eyewitnesses of incidents involving strange creatures in the lakes of Connemara. Local people have been (15) ________ not to swim in the lakes.

	A	B	C	D
0	A watched	B looked	C spotted	D reported
1	A bay	B beach	C coast	D shore
2	A inquiring	B searching	C investigating	D exploring
3	A recent	B last	C final	D these
4	A taken	B found	C seen	D got
5	A said	B told	C claimed	D described
6	A as	B like	C similar	D such
7	A distance	B distant	C further	D offshore
8	A believed	B checked	C repeated	D confirmed
9	A terrible	B terrified	C terrorized	D terrifying
10	A only	B similar	C just	D lot
11	A events	B information	C news	D details
12	A managed	B allowed	C able	D possible
13	A top	B waves	C surface	D depth
14	A suits	B matches	C goes	D reminds
15	A denied	B ordered	C informed	D warned

Exam practice: Use of English, Part 4

2 For questions 1–15, read the text below and look carefully at each line. Some of the lines are correct, and some have a word which should not be there. If a line is correct, put a tick (✓). If a line has a word which should not be there, write the word.

Is it a bird or is it a plane?

✓ 0 In 1655, a Portugese man appears to have been transported within
some 00 seconds from one country to another by some mysterious forces.
________ 1 The man was for doing business in the Portugese colony of Goa in
________ 2 India when suddenly he found himself back in Portugal. He was
________ 3 put on trial, which may or may not have been fair, and he was been
________ 4 condemned to death. The authorities in Portugal at the time tended to
________ 5 explain things according to their religious beliefs as well as and their
________ 6 knowledge of the world. Their world included witches, magicians and
________ 7 devils, who they were believed to be enemies of the Church and
________ 8 authority. One of the characteristics by which these evil creatures
________ 9 could have be recognized was that they were able to fly through the
________ 10 air. We do not know about whether the man from Goa was carried
________ 11 through the air or not. There are no surviving details of the case
________ 12 although that the evidence at the time was thought to be good enough
________ 13 to convict him. Since the seventeenth century, many other cases have
________ 14 been reported in the which people have claimed to have flown through
________ 15 the air. Nowadays most of people do not believe in witches and
magicians and UFOs are offered as an alternative explanation.

Exam practice: Use of English, Part 5

3 For questions 1–10, read the text below. Use the word given in capitals at the end of each line to form a word that fits in the space in the same line.

The men and women who vanish

We often read or hear about people (0) *disappearing* , some of	DISAPPEAR
whom come back again, while others vanish forever. It has been suggested	
that these people were taken by aliens; some go (1) __________ ,	WILL
while others are (2) __________ by the visitors from outer space.	KIDNAP
It is not surprising that those who do come back after a mysterious	
(3) __________ find it difficult to make people accept their	ABSENT
(4) __________ .	EXPLAIN
We can only wonder what has (5) __________ happened to those	REAL
who never return. There is one story from the nineteenth century of the	
(6) __________ of a certain Mr Rhys. When he failed to return after	DISAPPEAR
(7) __________ an evening in the company of a friend, and	SPEND
(8) __________ failed to discover him, his friend, John Davies, was	SEARCH
accused of (9) __________ him. Fortunately for Davies, there was	MURDER
a local farmer with a (10) __________ of such mysteries and this man	KNOW
persuaded everyone involved that Rhys had actually been taken away	
by alien creatures.	

The passive

Exam practice: Use of English, Part 3

4 For questions 1–10, complete the second sentence so that it has a similar meaning to the first sentence, using the word given. Do not change the word given. You must use between two and five words, including the word given.

0 My sister is not old enough to ride a bicycle.
too
My sister is ______ *too young to* ______ ride a bicycle.

1 You can't leave the room during the exam.
allowed
You ____________________ the room till the end of the exam.

2 The price of the room includes breakfast.
is
Breakfast ____________________ the price of the room.

3 Some people said Peter stole the pen.
accused
Peter ____________________ the pen by some people.

4 They haven't finished building the bridge yet.
completed
The ____________________ yet.

5 They will want to know what you have in your suitcase.
asked
You ____________________ show the contents of your suitcase.

6 The police are examining the case carefully.
looked
The case ____________________ carefully by the police.

7 They are not going to let him get away with his crimes.
punished
He is ____________________ his crimes.

8 It is possible that the cat got run over by a car.
killed
The cat ____________________ by a car.

9 The government has reduced income tax.
cut
Income tax ____________________ the government.

10 Don't let the children stay up too late.
allowed
The children ____________________ stay up too late.

5 Rewrite the newspaper headlines below using the correct passive form. Add words and use your own ideas to make complete sentences.

1 PENSIONER RUN OVER
A pensioner was run over in Banbury Road yesterday.

2 MAN STRUCK BY LIGHTNING IN FOREST
____

3 NEW SCHOOL TO BE OPENED BY MAYOR
____

4 WORLD RECORD BROKEN IN 100 METRES
____

5 WOMAN MURDERED IN WOODS ON EVENING STROLL
____

6 HOSPITAL TO CLOSE – LACK OF FUNDS
____

7 'CURE FOR CANCER IN FIVE YEARS,' SAYS RESEARCHER
____

8 TESTS MADE MORE DIFFICULT TO RAISE FALLING STANDARDS
____

9 ENGLISH SPOKEN BY ONE BILLION, CLAIMS REPORT
____

6 Complete this text using the correct passive form of one of the verbs below in each space. Use two of the verbs more than once.

refer use bring give invent write call beat build

Why does nothing exist?

Did nothing always exist or (1) *was* it *invented*? 'Nothing' is zero or nought (0). It is a very useful idea and it (2) __________ by many different names. In football, 0 (3) __________ to as 'nil'. So we say: 'Liverpool (4) __________ two-nil (2-0) at home by Manchester United.' When you (5) __________ marks in a test, you hope you will never get 'nought' out of ten or twenty. When we talk about the temperature, 'zero' (6) __________. We say: 'It is freezing today; the temperature has dropped to five below zero.' The most unusual name for 0 must be that which (7) __________ in tennis, 'love'; where the scoring goes 15-love, 30-love and so on. Not many people realize that 0 did not always exist but is something that had (8) __________. Until the sixteenth century, the number system used in Europe was the Roman system, which was invented about two thousand years ago. The Roman system is not simple, for example the mark 'X' stands for ten and 'C' refers to a hundred. A much better number system (9) __________ by the Hindus much earlier. The Hindu system (10) __________ to Europe in AD 900 by the Arabs and is sometimes referred to as the 'Arabic system'. This system (11) __________ on a base of ten and all numbers (12) __________ with the digits: 1, 2, 3, 4, 5, 6, 7, 8, 9 and 0. So as all schoolchildren know, 10 means 'ten' and 40 means 'four times ten'.

Adjective order

7 Put the adjectives given in brackets in the correct order.

1 We bought a/an ______________________________ table. (old/large/dining)
2 He bought her a/an ______________________________ vase. (antique/beautiful)
3 He gave her a/an ______________________________ ring. (gold/expensive)
4 He is a ______________________________ man. (dark/handsome/tall)
5 What a ______________________________ boy! (little/nice)
6 I always take a ______________________________ briefcase to work. (black/leather/large)
7 When I do the gardening, I always wear a/an ______________________________ jacket. (cotton/old/blue)
8 An ______________________________ knife. (old/hunting/Indian)
9 A ______________________________ knife. (bread/steel/stainless)
10 A ______________________________ waiter. (Chinese/fat/big)

VOCABULARY

Adjectives ending in *-ed* and *-ing*

1 Complete this table.

verb	noun	adjective (x 2)
amuse		
bore		
confuse		
depress		
disappoint		
disgust		
entertain		
excite		
exhaust		
fascinate		
frighten		
involve		
irritate		
puzzle		
satisfy		
shock		

Word formation

2 Solve the clues below to complete the crossword and to find the missing word.

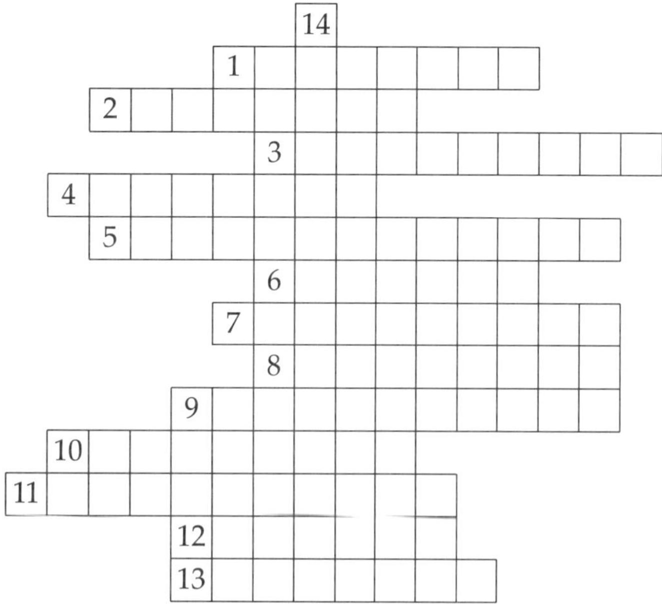

1 a person who plays the piano professionally
2 a person who cleans buildings
3 a person who plays the violin professionally
4 a person who helps you practise a sport
5 a person who tries to find out more about a crime
6 a person who types letters
7 Look it up in the telephone ________________ .
8 a person who looks after flowers and plants
9 a person who writes plays
10 a person who makes films or puts on plays
11 a machine used by six above
12 a person who buys Camels and Marlboro
13 a person who is in charge of a company or office
14 The missing word is ________________ .

Phrasal verbs with *look*

3 Complete these sentences using the correct form of one of the phrasal verbs below in each space. Use one of the phrasal verbs twice.

look up look out look forward to look into look out for look through look down on look after look back

1 They don't know how the accident happened; they are ___*looking into*___ it.
2 Could you ____________________ these old newspapers for articles about the environment?
3 I can never remember telephone numbers; I always have to ___________ them ___________ in the directory.
4 She is a snob – she ____________________ other people.
5 When we go on holiday, our neighbour ____________________ the cats for us.
6 ____________________ ! That flowerpot is going to fall off the window-ledge!
7 When you go to the conference, will you ____________________ Bill and give him my regards?
8 When I ____________________ to my school-days, I realize how lucky I was.
9 I am ____________________ receiving your letter.
10 I think we should ____________________ the subject a bit before we decide which computer to buy.

10 What's in a face?

GRAMMAR AND USE OF ENGLISH

Exam practice: Use of English, Part 2

1 For questions 1–15, read the text below and think of the word which best fits each space. Use only one word in each space.

Reading faces

Hippocrates, the father of medicine, believed (0) *that* personality and physical appearance (1) ____________ together. Even in our own times, researchers (2) ____________ tried to prove that a person's character is somehow connected (3) ____________ the way they look. Psychologists often divide people (4) ____________ two types: those that are short and fat and those that are tall and thin. People in the first group tend to be shorter (5) ____________ average and as they grow older they (6) ____________ fatter. Although, in general, these people tend to be cheerful extroverts, (7) ____________ mood may suddenly change and they become either depressed (8) ____________ inward-looking. Criminals often fall into this group and many dictators have also (9) ____________ of the short, stocky type, for (10) ____________ Nero, Napoleon and Mussolini. Tall, thin people usually (11) ____________ smallish heads, long noses and bony faces. As far (12) ____________ their personality is concerned, they tend to be both shy (13) ____________ bad-tempered. They often suffer (14) ____________ stress and avoid physical activity, although (15) ____________ they do take part in sports, they are generally very good.

Exam practice: Use of English, Part 4

2 For questions 1–15, read the text below and look carefully at each line. Some of the lines are correct, and some have a word which should not be there. If a line is correct, put a tick (✓). If a line has a word which should not be there, write the word.

Get your hair cut!

for 0 My mother was very interested for in my hair. She would watch it
✓ 00 growing very carefully until it had got to a length which she thought
________ 1 was scandalous. Then she would start hinting that it was time to
________ 2 must get it cut. In those days (I was a teenager then) I was very fond
________ 3 of my many hair. You might say I was very attached to it and I hated
________ 4 to be parted from it. The longer it grew, the better I felt it. My hair was
________ 5 thick and curly and I was afraid I would look ridiculous without it.
________ 6 When I was a little, women in the local corner shop used to admire
________ 7 it and wish they had hair like mine one; instead they had to go and
________ 8 have had their hair curled at the hairdresser's. I was therefore proud
________ 9 of my mop of black, curly hair. When I ignored about my mother's
________ 10 hints she would ask, tongue-in-cheek, whether I intended to
________ 11 become a pop singer or a priest. (Orthodox priests let their hair to

________ 12 grow long.) When her little jokes became threats and were combined
________ 13 with my father's commands to go and get off my hair cut without
________ 14 further delay, I gave them in. I would then spend a few months feeling
________ 15 miserable until my hair had grown. Then, once again, my mother would start complaining ...

Exam practice: Use of English, Part 5

3 For questions 1–10, read the text below. Use the word given in capitals at the end of each line to form a word that fits in the space in the same line.

Show me your face and I'll tell you who you are

People have for a long time held the (0) ___belief___ that the face	BELIEVE
is in some way a reflection of (1) __________ . There is nothing	PERSON
(2) __________ or mysterious about it: we all have different	MAGIC
physical (3) __________ and therefore our	CHARACTER
(4) __________ is unique. How you feel about yourself also has	APPEAR
a direct influence on your facial (5) __________ . If, for example, you	EXPRESS
have a lot of (6) self- __________ , this will show in your face.	CONFIDENT
From ancient times, this (7) __________ between particular	CONNECT
features and aspects of personality was made, and a systematic study of	
the (8) __________ developed and became known as *physiognomy*.	RELATE
Physiognomy has proved that people's faces (9) __________ reflect	ACCURATE
people's characters. For those who don't find the idea convincing, let us take	
the example of (10) __________ twins, who not only look alike but	IDENTITY
also behave in a similar way.	

Either ... or, both ... and, not only ... but also, neither ... nor

Exam practice: Use of English, Part 3

4 For questions 1–10, complete the second sentence so that it has a similar meaning to the first sentence, using the word given. Do not change the word given. You must use between two and five words, including the word given.

0 My sister is not old enough to ride a bicycle.
too
My sister is ___too young to___ ride a bicycle.

1 I did not enjoy the performance and I didn't like the theatre.
neither
I liked ____________________ the theatre.

2 She is mean and bad-tempered.
but
Not ____________________ she is also bad-tempered.

3 Both the corner shop and the supermarket have what we want.
shopping
We can ________________________________ the corner shop or at the supermarket.

4 They burgled the house and did a lot of damage too.
they
Not ________________________________ the house but they also did a lot of damage.

5 The food looks and smells good.
only
The food ________________________________ it also smells good.

6 I failed the test and so did John.
passed
Neither ________________________________ the test.

7 He is ambitious and he wants to make a lot of money.
get
Not only ________________________________ on but he wants to be rich as well.

8 Smoking cigarettes and pipes is not allowed during the flight.
either
They won't let you ________________________________ a pipe during the flight.

9 He is a good footballer but he is also a nice person.
play
Not only ________________________________ but he is also a nice person.

10 The two starters in the set menu are soup and salad.
either
There ________________________________ as a starter in the set menu.

Causative verbs

5 Are the statements below true of your country? Rewrite these sentences so they are true of your country.

1 When their car breaks down, most people repair it themselves.
____

2 Most men cook their own meals.
____

3 Most families have their milk delivered to their house.
____

4 If a pipe is leaking in the house, people mend it themselves.
____

5 Most people do their own housework.
____

6 Children in my country make their own beds.
____

6 Complete these sentences using the correct form of one of the verbs below in each space. Then match the sentences with the explanations below.

deliver develop paint cut repair take bring make test clean

1 He likes to have his breakfast ________________ to him in bed because ...
2 He is going to have his portrait ________________ because ...
3 She needs to have her eyes ________________ because ...
4 She has had the television ________________ because ...
5 He is having his hair ________________ on Saturday because ...
6 He is going to have a new suit ________________ because ...
7 She has the shopping ________________ to her house because ...
8 She wants to have her sofa professionally ________________ because ...
9 He is going to have his photograph ________________ because ...
10 He can't wait to have the film ________________ because ...

a ... he thinks he is very handsome.
b ... it takes ages to dry when he washes it.
c ... it looks old and dirty.
d ... he is looking forward to seeing his holiday snaps.
e ... the picture was a bit fuzzy.
f ... he is lazy.
g ... he is going to get married.
h ... he needs a new passport.
i ... she keeps bumping into things.
j ... she is too old to carry it.

VOCABULARY

Describing people

1 Underline the odd word out in each group.

1	**nose**	pointed	flat	straight	curly	long
2	**hair**	frizzy	deep	curly	wavy	straight
3	**ears**	small	sticking out	pointed	prominent	turned-up
4	**face**	long	round	low	pear-shaped	thin
5	**lips**	fleshy	full	thick	wavy	thin
6	**forehead**	prominent	round	high	low	wide
7	**body**	well-built	skinny	stocky	slim	bushy
8	**eyes**	slanting	round	close together	high	small

2 Solve the clues below to complete the crossword and to find the missing word.

1 Do you feel like this before an exam or a visit to the dentist?
2 People who get into fights very easily are ____________ .
3 Her face is shaped like a fruit, but it's not an apple.
4 He does a lot of body-building so he is very ____________ .
5 He's not thin, he's not fat, he's quite muscular – so he's ____________ .
6 Relax, you're too ____________ .
7 That was a very ____________ remark to make; I don't think you should have mentioned her divorce.
8 The opposite of *stupid* is ____________ .
9 If you have a broad, strong body, you are ____________ .
10 Anna is so ____________ ; she never thinks of anyone but herself.
11 The missing word is ____________ .

Phrasal verbs

3 Complete these sentences using the correct form of one of the phrasal verbs below in each space.

put on hold on put back take back get on hold back take on go back on go on get back

1 When you've finished playing with your toys, please ________ them ________ in the cupboard.
2 Did you ________ your money ________ off the travel agent when the holiday was cancelled?
3 Can you ____________ till I've finished talking to the manager? Then I'll be right with you.
4 You gave me your word. You can't ____________ it now.
5 Let's ____________ from where we left off. Where were we before we were interrupted?
6 I am determined to succeed – nothing in the world will ________ me ________ .
7 ____________ your nicest clothes because I'm taking you to the best restaurant in town.
8 I'm afraid I don't ____________ very well with the man who lives next door.
9 Hearing that song ________ me ________ to my university days; I haven't heard it for years.
10 If we ________ you ________ , will you be able to work on Saturdays?

11 Meat: to eat or not to eat?

GRAMMAR AND USE OF ENGLISH

Exam practice: Use of English, Part 1

1 For questions 1–15, read the text below and decide which answer A, B, C or D best fits each space.

A short history of beef

The word *beef*, which (0) ___B___ to the flesh of a cow or an ox, did not come to England with William the Conqueror, as many people believe: it was first (1) ________ over from France towards the (2) ________ of the thirteenth century. There are records of beef being eaten nearly 4 500 years ago and beef was the most (3) ________ food with the Romans when they (4) ________ in Britain. The Anglo Saxons (5) ________ to prefer mutton or pork, but the Normans were definitely (6) ________ on beef. The Normans also preferred cow's milk to sheep's milk and as a (7) ________ there was a steady rise in the number of cows in Britain, so that (8) ________ the thirteenth century beef had become the country's favourite meat. It has (9) ________ that position ever since and the 'roast beef of old England' has a special (10) ________ not only in the hearts of the English people but also in their (11) ________ , especially when beef is accompanied by Yorkshire pudding, a traditional English (12) ________ . The word *beef* has also acquired several metaphorical meanings in (13) ________ English. It can (14) ________ 'muscular power or effort', as in the adjective 'beefy' or to complain, as in 'Stop beefing about your job all the time.' Both of these uses of the word came (15) ________ from the United States in the nineteenth century.

	A	B	C	D
0	A means	B refers	C used	D names
1	A brought	B came	C taken	D fetched
2	A end	B finish	C conclusion	D final
3	A favourite	B tasty	C popular	D best
4	A arrived	B reached	C visited	D gone
5	A would	B had	C insisted	D tended
6	A fonder	B keener	C preferred	D enthusiastic
7	A conclusion	B rule	C result	D cause
8	A until	B at	C by	D on
9	A kept	B got	C been	D continued
10	A part	B situation	C piece	D place
11	A kitchen	B cook	C meal	D cuisine
12	A cooking	B plate	C food	D dish
13	A everyday	B today	C usual	D nowadays
14	A refer	B intend	C signal	D mean
15	A along	B to	C over	D round

Exam practice: Use of English, Part 4

2 For questions 1–15, read the text below and look carefully at each line. Some of the lines are correct, and some have a word which should not be there. If a line is correct, put a tick (✓). If a line has a word which should not be there, write the word.

The sandwich

___✓___ 0 John Montague, the eleventh Earl of Sandwich, was so keen
___the___ 00 on the gambling that he could not drag himself away from the
________ 1 card table, even for a meal. Once he has spent 24 hours playing
________ 2 cards without once getting up to eat or drink. Instead, to stop
________ 3 himself from feeling hungry during the game, he had his servants
________ 4 make to him a special 'portable' meal, made up of a piece of cold
________ 5 beef between two slices of a toast. There was nothing original
________ 6 in putting a piece of bread round vegetables or even if round a
________ 7 lump of meat. It had been done for as long as bread itself had
________ 8 existed. However, it was this famous incident that it gave the
________ 9 snack a name: the *sandwich*. The first written record we have of the
________ 10 use of the word in this sense goes back to 1762. The word was
________ 11 well off established by the middle of the nineteenth century and
________ 12 even began to be used as a verb whose meaning 'to put something
________ 13 between two things of another type', as in the, 'I found myself
________ 14 sandwiched between a crowd of football fans and a brick wall.'
________ 15 Also, someone who carries away two advertising boards over his
shoulders came to be known as a 'sandwich man'.

Exam practice: Use of English, Part 5

3 For questions 1–10, read the text below. Use the word given in capitals at the end of each line to form a word that fits in the space in the same line.

Eat more fruit and vegetables!

A recent report on the (0) ___eating___ habits of children in Britain	EAT
suggests that children from the age of three to sixteen show a	
strong (1) ________________ for vegetables and only eat	LIKE
(2) ________________ amounts of fruit and vegetables at Christmas.	SUFFICE
One researcher says not eating (3) ________________ may have	PROPER
serious consequences on a child's (4) ________________ and physical	SPEAK
development, resulting in poorer performance at school.	
One (5) ________________ is to give children extra iron and vitamins but	SOLVE
in the long run it is more (6) ________________ if children get the right	EFFECT
ingredients in their (7) ________________ diet.	DAY
(8) ________________ , parents choose food for their children that is	FORTUNATE
quick and (9) ________________ to prepare, rather than food which is fresh	CONVENIENCE
and healthy. (10) ________________ , it is difficult later to get children to	CONSEQUENCE
change their habits.	

Prepositions

Exam practice: Use of English, Part 3

4 For questions 1–10, complete the second sentence so that it has a similar meaning to the first sentence, using the word given. Do not change the word given. You must use between two and five words, including the word given.

0 My sister is not old enough to ride a bicycle.
too
My sister is ______too young to______ ride a bicycle.

1 The police accused him of stealing the wallet.
charged
He ______________________ stealing the wallet.

2 He would not stop talking although no one was listening.
insisted
He ______________________ although no one was listening.

3 I regret having to leave the party early.
apologize
I ______________________ to leave the party early.

4 If we have a discussion about the problem, we might find a solution.
discuss
If ______________________ we might find a solution.

5 The house was in darkness except for a light in the kitchen.
apart
The house was completely ______________________ a light in the kitchen.

6 I have had enough of tidying up after you every day.
tired
I ______________________ after you every day.

7 I've lost interest completely in lessons at school.
bored
I am ______________________ lessons at school.

8 They continued to look for the girl till it got dark.
search
The ______________________ on till it got dark.

9 The school's success in the FCE exam made everyone feel very proud.
proud
Everyone ______________________ the school's success in the FCE exam.

10 I respect you a lot.
respect
I have ______________________ you.

5 Complete this dialogue with an appropriate preposition in each space. Who do you think A, B and Tom are?

A: I wish you'd stop complaining (1) *about* all the work we have to do and get on with packing the suitcases.

B: I'm not packing because I'm annoyed (2) __________ you.

A: What are you accusing me (3) __________ now?

B: I'm not accusing you and you know I'm as anxious (4) __________ missing the plane as you are, but I insist (5) __________ discussing this problem now.

A: I don't know what you're talking (6) __________ and we don't have much time to think (7) __________ anything else now. The plane takes off in exactly two hours and I don't think it's going to wait (8) __________ us if we're not there one hour before. So what do you want to discuss?

B: Look, you know I have great admiration (9) __________ your ability to organize things and I admit you should be congratulated (10) __________ making all the arrangements for the trip.

A: Well, if you have such enormous respect (11) __________ my organizational skills, why don't you listen (12) __________ me and just get on with the packing? We're late enough as it is.

B: Well, let me just say this: you know how fond I am (13) __________ Tom ...

A: Tom? What has Tom got to do with it?

B: I know that Tom is closer (14) __________ me than he is to you, but still, aren't you afraid of what might happen to him while we're away?

A: Look – my love (15) __________ Tom is as great as yours and any threat (16) __________ him is a threat to me too. I'm as loyal (17) __________ him as you are and I object (18) __________ any suggestion that I don't care (19) __________ him.

B: OK, OK, I apologize (20) __________ saying you don't care (21) __________ Tom. I just want you to know I feel a bit scared (22) __________ what might happen.

A: Well, can we stop arguing (23) __________ it because I can't come up with a solution (24) __________ the problem now – we just don't have time.

B: Look, I know you're tired (25) __________ hearing me go on about this, but do you think we could slip him into one of our bags and take him with us?

6 Now complete this table.

verb	preposition	adjective	preposition	noun	preposition
complain	*about*	annoyed		admiration	
accuse		anxious		respect	
insist		fond		love	
talk		close		threat	
think		loyal		solution	
wait		scared			
congratulate		tired			
listen					
object					
care					
apologize					
argue					

VOCABULARY

Word formation

1 Match words from list A with words from list B to make compound nouns. Use some of the words more than once.

A	B	
grape	apple	________________
mashed	meat	________________
straw	beans	________________
fruit	berry	________________
beet	wine	________________
minced	salad	________________
roast	burger	________________
pork	fruit	________________
green	flakes	________________
beef	chop	________________
white	beef	________________
baked	water	________________
mineral	potatoes	________________
instant	root	________________
corn	cream	________________
French	coffee	________________
ice	fries	________________
pine		________________

Idioms with food words

2 Complete these idioms using one of the words below in each space.

bread meat cucumber peanuts bananas cake beetroot bean

1 I hardly paid anything for it; I got it for ________________ .
2 He went mad, completely ________________ !
3 It's worthless; it's not worth a ________________ .
4 He didn't lose his control at all. He stayed cool as a ________________ .
5 I make my living by doing private lessons; they're my ________________ and butter.
6 I was so embarrassed. I went as red as a ________________ .
7 I like a book with a lot of ________________ in it, like *War and Peace*.
8 It's so easy; it's a piece of ________________ .

Phrasal verbs

3 Replace the underlined words in these sentences with the correct form of one of the phrasal verbs below. Make any other changes that are necessary.

give up **give away** **run out** **cut down** **cut up** **put on** **put off**

1 I am going to stop eating meat after all these stories about mad cows.

____

2 I am two kilos heavier than I was last year.

____

3 Before you put the meat in the pan you have to chop it into little pieces.

____

4 We haven't got any milk left.

____

5 I didn't want the kids' old toys so I donated them to a charity.

____

6 Your bad opinion of the film has made me not want to go and see it.

____

7 I am going to eat less sugar from now on.

____

12 The power and magic of dreams

GRAMMAR AND USE OF ENGLISH

Exam practice: Use of English, Part 2

1 For questions 1–15, read the text below and think of the word which best fits each space. Use only one word in each space.

The world of dreams 1

Most people feel that when they dream, they (0) ____are____ carried off to another world. (1) __________ the contrary, dreams are often connected (2) __________ our daily lives. (3) __________ our whole mind (4) __________ filled with something, when we are either very upset (5) __________ when we are in good spirits, a dream will represent (6) __________ reality in symbols. It is often said that we benefit (7) __________ dreams because they help the spirit to heal itself when things (8) __________ wrong. Dreams are therefore (9) __________ kind of escape, almost a holiday from (10) __________ life, with its fears and responsibilities. It is, (11) __________ , a strange (12) __________ of holiday because whether we have a wonderful time or whether it turns (13) __________ to be a nightmare, we quickly forget it. Most dreams disappear forever, (14) __________ you are one of those people disciplined enough to write (15) __________ down as soon as you wake up.

Exam practice: Use of English, Part 4

2 For questions 1–15, read the text below and look carefully at each line. Some of the lines are correct, and some have a word which should not be there. If a line is correct, put a tick (✓). If a line has a word which should not be there, write the word.

Bruce's dream

___✓___ 0 Bruce came over to my table at breakfast and asked whether he
___to___ 00 could to join me. Without waiting for my reply, he sat down and
_______ 1 within seconds started telling me about the dream he had been had
_______ 2 the night before. I really wanted to have a quiet breakfast without
_______ 3 talking much, but I muttered a polite 'That's interesting' as Bruce
_______ 4 explained that he had had dreamt that he was a pilot and was flying
_______ 5 some passengers to a remote holiday destination in the Bahamas.
_______ 6 I told him I needed some and more coffee because I found it difficult
_______ 7 to wake me up otherwise and have a proper conversation. He
_______ 8 carried on with the next episode of his dream which, he said, was
_______ 9 the most interesting part. One of the passengers had turned out to
_______ 10 be a terrorist and had hijacked the plane. Bruce explained me that he
_______ 11 had been reading a book about a hijack and he said the dream must

_______ 12 have come about as a result of this. He also told me he was too
_______ 13 scared of flying. I tried to change the subject by asking if he was
_______ 14 planning to go anywhere interesting in the summer and that was my
_______ 15 most big mistake. He went on to tell me in great detail that his dream
had always been to visit the Bahamas. He asked whether I had ever
been to the Caribbean and explained that it wasn't really all that expensive.

Exam practice: Use of English, Part 5

3 For questions 1–10, read the text below. Use the word given in capitals at the end of each line to form a word that fits in the space in the same line.

The world of dreams 2

While some dreams (0) *disappear* forever, other dreams come	APPEAR
back again and again, which for the (1) __________ is like going	DREAM
back to the same place for a (2) __________ and doing the same	VACATE
things. We do not only 'go back' to (3) __________ experiences	ENJOY
but also to (4) __________ ones. An example of a nice dream is	PLEASURE
when we are doing something very (5) __________ , like winning	SUCCESS
a prize, while a common nightmare is when we are making fools	
of (6) __________ in public or being in a situation from which it is	SELF
(7) __________ to escape. Perhaps, then, we should not see	POSSIBLE
dreams as an escape from (8) __________ , but as an extension	REAL
of it. In dreams, we (9) __________ continue to occupy ourselves	USUAL
with whatever pleasure or problems we have had during the day, while we	
were (10) __________ . So, rather than freeing us from everyday	WAKE
life, dreams lead us back to it.	

Reported speech and reported questions

4 Complete this dialogue, which is based on the text in exercise 2. Use between one and four words in each space.

Bruce: Ah, good morning Mary. Mind if I (1) ______________ ? Thanks.
Mary: I was just finishing my breakfast.
Bruce: You know, I (2) ______________ the strangest dream last night.
Mary: Oh, really.
Bruce: Shall I tell you about it? Well, I dreamt that I was a pilot and I (3) ______________ this plane, you see, to the Bahamas.
Mary: How interesting. I could do with another cup of coffee. I (4) ______________ difficult to have a proper conversation if I (5) ______________ enough coffee inside me, don't you?
Bruce: Yes. The next part of the dream (6) ______________ interesting part. You see, one of the passengers (7) ______________ to be a terrorist and he (8) ______________ the plane.
Mary: You don't say!
Bruce: Yes, you see, I (9) ______________ this book about terrorism and I reckon that's why I

(10) ____________ this dream, don't you? They say dreams are just a continuation of our everyday life, you know. And shall I tell you something else? (11) ____________ pretty scared of flying. Bet you didn't know that.

Mary: No. (12) ____________ to go anywhere interesting for your holidays this summer?

Bruce: Well, Mary, it's interesting you should ask me that because, you know what? My dream (13) ____________ to visit the Bahamas.

Mary: Really.

Bruce: (14) ____________ to the Caribbean? It's not really all that expensive, you know. What are you doing this summer, by the way?

Exam practice: Use of English, Part 3

5 For questions 1–10, complete the second sentence so that it has a similar meaning to the first sentence, using the word given. Do not change the word given. You must use between two and five words, including the word given.

0 My sister is not old enough to ride a bicycle.
too
My sister is ____too young to____ ride a bicycle.

1 'I did not steal the money from the till,' said the boy.
stolen
The boy ____________ the money from the till.

2 'I have never killed anyone,' said the accused.
ever
The accused denied that he ____________ anyone.

3 'Who ate the cake?' she asked.
had
She wanted ____________ the cake.

4 'Freud's book was not the first one about dreams,' said the lecturer.
written
The lecturer explained that books about dreams ____________ Freud's book.

5 'Do you ever have nightmares in which you're falling from a great height?'
dreamt
She asked him whether ____________ about falling from a great height.

6 'He must pay his bill soon,' said Jill.
pay
She said ____________ his bill soon.

7 The psychiatrist asked her what she had dreamt about the night before.
dream
'What ____________ night?, asked the psychiatrist.

8 'You mustn't work so hard,' said the doctor to Katy.
not
The doctor advised ____________ hard.

9 He promised he would come on time in future.
late
'I promise I ________________________________ now on,' he said.

10 She asked them the way to the station.
way
'Could ________________________________ to the station?' she asked.

6 Complete these sentences using reported speech.

	Direct speech	Reported speech
1	'It is hot.'	Mary said ________________
2	'I saw Bruce.'	Mary told us ________________
3	'I've eaten.'	He said ________________
4	'I've been reading a good book.'	She said ________________
5	'I can sing.'	She claimed ________________
6	'You must rest.'	The doctor said ________________
7	'I saw him yesterday.'	She told us she ________________
8	'He hasn't been here today.'	She told us he ________________
9	'I'll give you the money tomorrow.'	He promised ________________
10	'Come here.'	He told her ________________
11	'Don't smoke.'	She told him ________________
12	'Do you smoke?'	She asked me ________________
13	'Are you coming or not?'	She asked me ________________
14	'Where do you come from?'	She asked me ________________

VOCABULARY

Phrasal verbs with *bring*

1 Replace the underlined words in these sentences with the correct form of one of the phrasal verbs below. Make any other changes that are necessary. Use each phrasal verb twice.

bring out **bring off** **bring up** **bring down** **bring back**

1 Isn't Michael Jackson going to release any more albums?
____

2 The government are trying to make the price of houses cheaper.
____

3 It was very difficult to swim across the English Channel but he managed it.
____

4 Do you believe they should re-introduce school uniforms?
____

5 The party wants to win the election for a fourth time. Do you think they can manage it?
____

6 Where did you spend your childhood?
____

7 Unpopular economic policies forced the government to resign.

____

8 Who mentioned the subject at the meeting?

____

9 My parents went to Australia for a holiday and they got me this boomerang as a souvenir.

____

10 The Japanese keep producing new electronic gadgets.

____

Word formation

2 Complete this table. Use the prefixes and suffixes to make as many adjectives as you can.

verb	noun	adjective (*un-*, *in-*, *ir-*, *-able*, *-ive*, *-ary*, *-ible*)
believe		
create		
desire		
explain		
express		
imagine		
interpret		
predict		
produce		
punish		
relate		
respond		
revolt		
value		

3 Complete these sentences using one of the words above in each space.

1 I am not going to clean the floor; it's not my ______________ .
2 Your ______________ for not doing your homework will be to stay behind after school.
3 I want to be a painter or a composer. I want to do something ______________ with my life.
4 The Queen of England's art collection is so ______________ that it is impossible to insure it.
5 He says he saw some visitors from outer space in his garden – it's just ______________ !
6 My husband's mood is very ______________ ; sometimes he's happy and the next minute he's depressed.
7 The French ______________ , which took place in 1789, changed the history of Europe.
8 He has a sad ______________ on his face. I wonder what's wrong?

13 Goodies and baddies

GRAMMAR AND USE OF ENGLISH

Exam practice: Use of English, Part 1

1 For questions 1–15, read the text below and decide which answer A, B, C or D best fits each space.

Police seek robbery link

A woman aged 68 (0) __B__ broken ribs in an attack by an armed robber in her penthouse in Kensington, London, police said yesterday. Police are (1) ________ at other robberies to see if they are linked after Rachael Avitan was (2) ________ at her home in Oxford Square. Mrs Avitan, the wife of a millionaire shipowner, was (3) ________ to open a safe before she was locked in the bathroom with the 24-year-old maid.

The robber escaped with jewellery, (4) ________ coins and cash. Police said the objects and money (5) ________ in the raid were worth about 30 000 pounds. They ruled out the (6) ________ that the raid was by a gang which (7) ________ its victims from *Who's Who* (a reference guide containing information (8) ________ important people), though Scotland Yard said it was possible a (9) ________ of robbers were targeting wealthy families living in Kensington, Belgravia and Chelsea. A (10) ________ for Scotland Yard said there may have been only one man behind the latest (11) ________ but it is not clear if it was one of a (12) ________ . Mrs Avitan has been allowed to leave hospital but is still having treatment for her (13) ________ . She said the robber broke in through the back door as her maid was letting herself out to go home. The man (14) ________ the maid and pulled her back into the house. He told Mrs Avitan she wouldn't get hurt if she (15) ________ over her valuables. 'It was terribly scary,' said Mrs Avitan.

	A	B	C	D
0	A caught	B suffered	C injured	D hurt
1	A searching	B examining	C looking	D inquiring
2	A kidnapped	B stolen	C attacked	D mugged
3	A forced	B pushed	C attacked	D threatened
4	A worthy	B costly	C expensive	D valuable
5	A escaping	B robbed	C missing	D taken
6	A belief	B chance	C possibility	D probability
7	A picks	B spots	C discovers	D checks
8	A for	B about	C around	D upon
9	A pack	B party	C pair	D team
10	A spokesperson	B speaker	C commentator	D presenter
11	A event	B attack	C fact	D robber
12	A collection	B team	C serial	D series
13	A pains	B aches	C wounds	D injuries
14	A took	B grabbed	C hugged	D squeezed
15	A gave	B handed	C took	D got

Exam practice: Use of English, Part 4

2 For questions 1–15, read the text below and look carefully at each line. Some of the lines are correct, and some have a word which should not be there. If a line is correct, put a tick (✓). If a line has a word which should not be there, write the word.

Made of money?

have	0	A couple were walking down Oxford Street when they have stopped
✓	00	to look in a jeweller's window. The woman, who was young and
________	1	attractive but a little bit also vain, said she'd love to have a pair of
________	2	diamond ear-rings. The man, who was not very well off, was madly
________	3	in love with the girl and didn't want to lose her. Suddenly he did took
________	4	a brick out of his pocket, smashed the window and grabbed the
________	5	ear-rings, then which he gave to the woman. She gave him a big hug
________	6	and a smile and they carried on walking. A little further down the
________	7	street they stopped at again another jeweller's and the woman saw
________	8	a beautiful diamond ring which she said she would love to have on
________	9	her finger. The man took up another brick from his pocket, smashed
________	10	a hole in the glass, grabbed at the ring and handed it to the woman,
________	11	who was, of course, too delighted. A few minutes later, they found
________	12	themselves standing outside yet another jeweller's window and
________	13	the woman looked at a pearl necklace of which she said would look
________	14	gorgeous round her neck. The man turned round angrily to the woman
________	15	and said: 'That's enough, you must think I'm made of bricks.'

Exam practice: Use of English, Part 5

3 For questions 1–10, read the text below. Use the word given in capitals at the end of each line to form a word that fits in the space in the same line.

Smuggler's reduced sentence

A British man was convicted and sentenced to twenty years'	
(0) *imprisonment* yesterday after a court in the northern city of	PRISON
Thessaloniki in Greece found him (1) ________________ of trying to	GUILT
smuggle ten kilograms of Turkish heroin into Greece.	
David Murray, who is (2) ________________ and a father of a young boy,	EMPLOY
was arrested last September on the Greek-Turkish border after	
special police (3) ________________ discovered the heroin in his car.	INVESTIGATE
A court spokesman said that Murray, a (4) ________________ of	RESIDE
Manchester in England, told the court that he had been hired to	
deliver the car from England to a (5) ________________ in Turkey. He	DESTINY
said he had accepted the job because he (6) ' ________________	DESPERATE
needed the money'. Once in Turkey, his (7) ' ________________ ' asked	EMPLOY
him to take the car to Greece. Murray was not given an	

(8) ________________ for this change of plan, but did it anyway. EXPLAIN
Murray's (9) ________________ managed to persuade the court to give LAW
him the reduced sentence of twenty years because he has not been
involved in a (10) ________________ activity before. CRIME

Used to/would + infinitive, *be/get used to* + *-ing*; relative clauses

Exam practice: Use of English, Part 3

4 For questions 1–10, complete the second sentence so that it has a similar meaning to the first sentence, using the word given. Do not change the word given. You must use between two and five words, including the word given.

0 My sister is not old enough to ride a bicycle.
too
My sister is ______too young to______ ride a bicycle.

1 I wish I knew the owner of this car.
whose
I wish ________________________________ is.

2 Driving on the right is a new experience for me.
used
I ________________________________ on the right.

3 There was a time when people didn't watch TV.
use
Years ago, people ________________________________ TV.

4 His father would disappear for days.
habit
His father had ________________________________ for days.

5 Our part of town has a serious crime problem.
neighbourhood
We live ________________________________ has a serious crime problem.

6 I haven't always smoked so much.
use
I ________________________________ so much.

7 I find it difficult to adjust to living here.
get
I ________________________________ living here.

8 We went to the seaside every summer when I was a child.
would
When I was a child, ________________________________ the seaside every summer.

9 Learning Chinese isn't so difficult for me now.
getting
I ________________________________ Chinese.

10 I went to school in this building.
used
This is the building ________________________________ to school.

5 Respond to these questions using *used to* + infinitive.

1 Murderers are not executed nowadays, are they?

____

2 Few children work in factories today, is that right?

____

3 There are more beggars on the streets than there were twenty years ago, don't you agree?

____

4 Are drug-related crimes more common nowadays?

____

5 There aren't so many hijackings now, are there?

____

6 Do you remember there being so many bank robberies when you were young?

____

7 You don't hear about pirates attacking ships much nowadays, do you?

____

8 Did you like stories about smugglers when you were a child?

____

VOCABULARY

Crime

1 Complete these definitions of words associated with crime with an appropriate relative pronoun.

1 a crime in *which* someone tries to get money out of someone else by threatening to make known something unpleasant = *blackmail*
2 to take control of an aircraft illegally, __________ you then use to achieve political aims = __________
3 a person __________ robs someone with violence in the street = __________
4 a building __________ people __________ have done wrong are kept locked up = __________
5 a small room in a prison __________ prisoners are kept = __________
6 a sum of money __________ is paid as a punishment = __________
7 a crime __________ involves killing a person intentionally = __________
8 a criminal act in __________ someone lights a fire in order to cause damage = __________
9 a person __________ should be blamed for a crime = __________
10 a person __________ commits a crime, often as an occupation = __________
11 a person __________ job it is to investigate a crime = __________
12 a person __________ job is to protect a person or a place = __________
13 a building __________ the police have their offices = __________

14 a small group of policemen ___________ work together = _______________
15 the area ___________ a policeman regularly works = _______________
16 a group of people (twelve in England) ___________ decide whether someone is innocent or guilty = _______________
17 a person ___________ business is to advise people about the law = _______________
18 a place ___________ criminal cases are heard = _______________
19 the closed area in a court ___________ the prisoner is kept = _______________
20 anything ___________ helps to prove something in a court of law = _______________

Now match the words from the box with the definitions above.

fine	court	beat	blackmail	evidence	murder	guard	mugger	criminal	squad
cell	lawyer	detective	station	dock	culprit	hijack	arson	jury	prison

2 Complete these sentences using one of the words from the box above in each space.

1 I want to speak to my _______________ before I sign these papers.
2 The accused was set free because there was a lack of _______________ .
3 Small political groups often _______________ planes in order to make their cause known to the world.
4 The prisoner escaped while the _______________ was sleeping.
5 He threatened to _______________ his boss by revealing his illegal behaviour to the press.
6 All the members of the _______________ decided the accused was guilty.
7 The old lady was attacked by a _______________ on her way home and robbed of her savings.
8 'I'd like you to come along to the police _______________ to answer some questions,' the police officer said.
9 He had to pay a _______________ of 50 pounds for speeding.
10 Someone has burgled their flat. The _______________ must be someone who knows the family well.

Word formation

3 Complete this table.

verb	**noun**	**verb**	**noun**
accuse		invest	
appear		occur	
assassinate		participate	
commit		produce	
confirm		prosecute	
educate		punish	
encourage		receive	
improoo		rob	
imprison		select	
improve		suspect	

4 Complete these sentences using the correct form of one of the words from the table in exercise 3 in each space.

1 Because of the ________________ of my teacher, I have decided to become a professional pianist.
2 If you ________________ a crime, you will be punished.
3 A bank ________________ took place on High Street yesterday.
4 What time did the burglary ________________ ?
5 The suspect will make an ________________ in court tomorrow.
6 The ________________ of President Kennedy took place in 1963.
7 The ________________ for murder is life ________________ .
8 ________________ should not stop after school, but should continue through your life.
9 ________________ in team sports is compulsory in my school.
10 To ________________ your skills in speaking English, you should practise as often as possible.

Phrasal verbs with *make* and *take*

5 Complete these exchanges using the correct form of one of the phrasal verbs below in each space. Use some of the phrasal verbs more than once.

make for take for make out take out make up take up make off take off

1 Who is on the committee?
It is ____________________ of two men and two women.
2 Why didn't you start French lessons last month?
I was too busy and I thought it would ____________________ too much time.
3 Did you go round the museum yesterday?
Yes, but I couldn't ____________________ what the guide was saying because it was all in French.
4 Why are you going to the dentist?
Because I have to have a couple of teeth ____________________ .
5 What do your students do at the end of the lesson?
They just grab their bags and ____________________ the door.
6 How much did the thieves get away with?
Oh, they must have ____________________ with at least one million pounds.
7 When did he become famous?
His career really ____________________ when he appeared in a film with Tom Hanks.
8 Did the jury believe the witness?
No, they thought he had ____________________ the whole story.
9 Hello, John.
I'm not John, I'm Charles.
Sorry, I ________ you ________ someone else.
10 What did you do on your birthday?
My parents ________ me ________ for a meal in an expensive restaurant.
11 How did you manage to avoid taking the test?
Easy. I just ____________________ I was ill.
12 Bruce and Mary have had a quarrel.
Yes, but I think they've kissed and ____________________ now.

14 TV times

GRAMMAR AND USE OF ENGLISH

Exam practice: Use of English, Part 2

1 For questions 1–15, read the text below and think of the word which best fits each space. Use only one word in each space.

TV choice

Grandstand (BBC 1, 10.55 am) In today's programme you can join Steve Rider for a morning session of snooker coming (0) ___from___ the Crucible Theatre in Sheffield. If you prefer something (1) ______ a bit more action, then stay switched (2) ______ for the Rugby League Cup Final (3) ______ St Helen's (the favourites) and the Bradford Bulls, which (4) ______ be broadcast live from Wembley at 2.30 pm.

FDR: Fear Itself (BBC 2, 8.05 pm) This is (5) ______ second in a four-part series (6) ______ the life of American President Franklin D Roosevelt. Tonight's episode looks at the period in Roosevelt's life when he contracted polio, a disease (7) ______ would have put an end to most careers, let alone that (8) ______ a man who was hoping to become President of the United States. This fascinating documentary shows (9) ______ Roosevelt fought back with great determination and optimism and not (10) ______ got back on his feet again, but also walked triumphantly (11) ______ the White House.

You ANC Nothing Yet (Channel 4, 12.05 am) This is an opportunity to enjoy a one-off performance (12) ______ Pieter-Dirk Uys, the Jewish-Afrikaner comedian (13) ______ satire has long been a thorn in the side of South Africa's political leaders, all of (14) ______ he makes fun of, although he admits he (15) ______ difficulty with his Nelson Mandela impression.

Exam practice: Use of English, Part 4

2 For questions 1–15, read the text below and look carefully at each line. Some of the lines are correct, and some have a word which should not be there. If a line is correct, put a tick (✓). If a line has a word which should not be there, write the word.

Overnight success

___been___ 0 A girl of ten has been become famous overnight after she was chosen
___✓___ 00 to play a leading role in a major film. Alice Coulthard, who lives in Muswell
______ 1 Hill, was spotted by a talent scouts at a drama school in Hornsey. Now
______ 2 she has been being asked to play one of the four children in the film
______ 3 *The Cement Garden*, which is based on the book by Ian McEwan. In the
______ 4 film she will to play the part of a twelve-year-old, locked away in her own
______ 5 world of books and thoughts. Alice's parents are delighted. 'We had a
______ 6 few doubts about at first, but now we are very pleased,' said her
______ 7 40-year-old father, Michael, a computer manager. *The Cement Garden*
______ 8 which has been turned into a screenplay by director and screenwriter

_________ 9 Andrew Birkin, who wrote *The Lost Boys*, an award-winning BBC series.
_________ 10 Producer Ene Vanaveski who said: 'We went to all the theatre schools,
_________ 11 but when we saw Alice she was just the right for the part.' Mr Birkin said
_________ 12 he was impressed by both of Alice's acting skills and her natural, unspoilt
_________ 13 personality. Alice has been taking on drama lessons for three years,
_________ 14 though she has been interested in acting since she was five. She has now
_________ 15 got her own agent and has started to go to other auditions.

Exam practice: Use of English, Part 5

3 For questions 1–10, read the text below. Use the word given in capitals at the end of each line to form a word that fits in the space in the same line.

Kids watch more TV

A study into children's television (0) ___*viewing*___ habits reveals	VIEW
that children whose parents have a high level of (1) _______________	EDUCATE
tend to watch less television than children from less educated	
family (2) _______________ . The report also suggests that a high rate	BACK
of TV watching amongst children in poorer (3) _______________ areas	SUBURB
and in the provinces, compared to those living in large urban centres, is	
often due to (4) _______________ and a lack of other kinds of	POOR
(5) _______________ in the area. Discos, cinema, theatre and sports	ENTERTAIN
(6) _______________ offer children in urban centres a wider range of	ACTIVE
pastimes, which leads to far (7) _______________ hours being spent	FEW
in front of the box. (8) _______________ , comedies and adventure	COMMERCE
films are children's (9) _______________ programmes, while twenty	FAVOUR
per cent of children said they preferred (10) _______________ films	VIOLENCE
and thrillers.	

Verbs followed by infinitive or *-ing* form (gerund)

Exam practice: Use of English, Part 3

4 For questions 1–10, complete the second sentence so that it has a similar meaning to the first sentence, using the word given. Do not change the word given. You must use between two and five words, including the word given.

0 My sister is not old enough to ride a bicycle.
too
My sister is ___*too young to*___ ride a bicycle.

1 This TV is too expensive for us to buy at the moment.
afford
We ___can't afford to buying___ this TV at the moment.
to buy

2 Peter's idea was to stay in and watch a movie on TV.
suggested
Peter ______________________________ a movie on TV.

3 She forgot to post the letter.
remember
She ______________________________ the letter.

4 I will never forget lying on the beach in Mykonos.
always
I ______________________________ on the beach in Mykonos.

5 I am not on speaking terms with Bruce.
stopped
I ______________________________ to Bruce.

6 I talked to Mary and then went home.
stopped
On the way home ______________________________ to Mary.

7 Unfortunately, you have not passed the test.
regret
We ______________________________ have not passed the test.

8 I wish I had married Mary!
regret
I ______________________________ Mary.

9 We could hear voices next door.
talking
We ______________________________ next door.

10 I'd appreciate it if you were a bit quieter.
try
Could ______________________________ less noise, please?

5 Complete these sentences with an appropriate verb or verb phrase.

1 I walked round the ladder because I wanted to ______________ walking under it.
2 Those shoes are much too expensive; we can't ______________ to pay that much.
3 I ______________ waiting in queues. It's one of the things I hate most.
4 ________ you ________ carrying this box? It's too heavy for me.
5 Simon and I have ______________ to get married this year.
6 I really ______________ lying on the beach reading a book. It's great!
7 She ______________ to bring her sun cream, so she's sure to get sunburn.
8 Can I ______________ banning smoking in the office? I think it would be better for everyone.
9 It's not ______________ paying that much money for a bit of plastic.
10 ________ you ________ to follow me, please? The manager is ready to see you.

6 Complete this letter using the correct form (infinitive with *to* or *-ing* form) of one of the verbs below in each space. Use two of the verbs twice.

ask **hear** **have** **see** **read** **travel** **make** **come** **arrive** **learn**

Dear Henry,

Thanks for your letter, which I enjoyed (1) ______________ very much. I am glad you will be able (2) ______________ to our conference in October and we are particularly pleased (3) ______________ you as our guest speaker. We are all looking forward to (4) ______________ you speak after (5) ______________ so many of your books over the years. I am sorry (6) ______________ that your wife Deborah is not well and will not be able to come, but we hope (7) ______________ her on a future occasion.

I would also like (8) ______________ you when you would prefer (9) ______________ , so I can arrange your flight for you. Please let me know as soon as you can when you intend (10) ______________ and leave. If you would prefer (11) ______________ these arrangements yourself, please let me know in the next few days.

I look forward to (12) ______________ from you,

Best wishes,

Luke

Ellipsis

7 Complete these sentences with an appropriate modal verb.

1 If you can't do it, we'll have to find someone who ___*can*___ .

2 You should have become a doctor.
You're right. I __________ have.

3 I have never stolen any money and I never __________ .

4 She is not as hard working as she __________ be.

5 He can sing much better than you __________ .

6 I didn't go to the dentist but now I realize I __________ have.

7 They are not yet rich and perhaps they never __________ be.

8 I would stop smoking if I __________ .

8 Complete these sentences with an appropriate auxiliary verb.

1 My mother has a job and so __________ my father.

2 Mary has decided to marry Arthur. Yes, I know she __________ .

3 I think you're taller than me. I'm sure I __________ .

4 Some students managed to pass the test, but others __________ .

5 They haven't visited the Parthenon yet, __________ they?

6 I think I eat more than you __________ .

7 She's probably got a lot of money. Yes, she certainly looks as if she __________ .

8 I'm absolutely exhausted. I thought you might __________ .

VOCABULARY

Television

1 Underline the odd word out in each group.

1 producer	director	channel	publisher
2 presenter	newscaster	printer	broadcast
3 episode	series	edition	soap
4 switch	turn	volume	box office
5 article	cartoon	comedy	newsflash
6 viewer	conductor	audience	quiz
7 repeat	announcer	drama	column

2 Complete this dialogue using one of the words from exercise 1 in each space.

Robert: (1) ________________ the television on, Marion. *The Rich and the Ugly* is on in a minute

Marion: You're not watching that rubbish, are you? I can't stand Brazilian (2) ________________ operas. Anyway, which (3) ________________ is it on?

Robert: I think it's on Channel Five. I only started watching it last week, this is the last (4) ________________ . I find it quite funny, more like a (5) ________________ than the usual melodramatic stuff.

Marion: I'd rather watch a (6) ________________ like *Tom and Jerry* or *The Flintstones* any day.

Robert: It's an incredibly popular (7) ________________ . It's got bigger (8) ________________ ratings than any other show on TV.

Marion: You mean to say that more (9) ________________ watch rubbish like that than any other programme?

Robert: Yes. Ah, it's just starting. Can you turn the (10) ________________ up? I can't hear anything.

Word formation

3 Complete this table using the suffixes *-al*, *-ic*, *-ous* and *-ful*.

noun	adjective	noun	adjective
athlete		harm	
care		history	
centre		humour	
comedy		origin	
danger		poison	
drama		practice	
education		science	
environment		tradition	
experiment		use	

4 Complete these sentences using one of the adjectives from the table in exercise 3 in each space.

1 Fortunately, there are few ________________ snakes in our country.
2 They will have to carry out a lot of ________________ experiments to find a cure for the disease.
3 Does watching violence on TV have a/an ________________ effect on children?
4 In the morning, some TV channels show ________________ programmes, which can help children with their school subjects.
5 Pollution, traffic and other ________________ problems are getting worse all the time.
6 The first landing on the Moon was a/an ________________ event.
7 Be ________________ when you answer the question in the exam and remember to check your answers.
8 The teacher made a/an ________________ remark and we all laughed.
9 What I like about the Olympics are the ________________ events, such as running and jumping.
10 The picture you see here is only a copy. The ________________ painting is in the Louvre.

Expressions and phrasal verbs with *keep*

5 Complete these sentences using one of the words or prepositions below in each space. Use one of the prepositions twice.

on diary back warm awake off word change secret up still

1 I gave the waiter five pounds and told him to keep the ________________ .
2 It's difficult to keep ________________ in this cold weather.
3 Keep ________________ while I take your picture – stop moving!
4 The noise from the party kept me ________________ all night.
5 I keep a ________________ because I like to write down what happens everyday.
6 He said he would marry me and he kept his ________________ .
7 He kept ________________ interrupting me. It was very rude.
8 Can you keep a ________________ ? You won't tell anyone?
9 She hasn't told us the whole story; I'm sure she's keeping something ________________ .
10 This is hard work. I can't keep it ________________ for long.
11 Traffic in most countries has to keep ________________ the right.
12 Notices warned us to keep ________________ the grass.

15 The end of intelligence?

GRAMMAR AND USE OF ENGLISH

Exam practice: Use of English, Part 1

1 For questions 1–15, read the text below and decide which answer A, B, C or D best fits each space.

What is genius?

When some psychiatrists attempt to explain genius, they talk in (0) __C__ of mental disturbance. This is a strange way of describing remarkable men. (Sadly, it is usually men, (1) ________ occasionally women are also mentioned.) Psychiatrists often (2) ________ to geniuses as people who (3) ________ to be oversensitive, melancholy and even schizophrenic; they channel their destructive energy into their masterpieces. A survey (4) ________ out on 30 American writers revealed that 37% of them (5) ________ from depression. A British study of famous artists (including poets, painters and sculptors) showed that 38% had (6) ________ some sort of psychiatric treatment.

An alternative (7) ________ of intelligence, expressed at a recent conference in the French city of Bordeaux, (8) ________ geniuses as people who matured very early and are workaholics with an amazing (9) ________ to produce a lot of work in a (10) ________ space of time: Bach, for example, with his 46 volumes of musical compositions. Does this mean intelligence and (11) ________ genius is a question of how much is created? We don't know the answer yet, but Thomas Edison, one of the greatest inventors (12) ________ all time, said that genius is 1% inspiration and 99% perspiration!

Other interesting (13) ________ about geniuses are that they tend to be born in Spring, (14) ________ Leonardo and Shakespeare, and they become orphans in their early childhood. One (15) ________ whether it is a sign of good or bad luck to be born a genius.

	A	B	C	D
0	A words	B explanations	C terms	D ways
1	A despite	B though	C however	D moreover
2	A talk	B speak	C mention	D refer
3	A tend	B used	C use	D will
4	A taken	B made	C carried	D put
5	A lived	B suffered	C passed	D been
6	A given	B taken	C received	D got
7	A view	B aspect	C research	D reason
8	A thinks	B believes	C sees	D take
9	A skill	B wish	C plan	D ability
10	A quick	B short	C soon	D bit
11	A still	B yet	C also	D even
12	A of	B in	C at	D from
13	A events	B facts	C knowledge	D problems
14	A like	B such	C as	D example
15	A asks	B thinks	C wonders	D denies

Exam practice: Use of English, Part 4

2 For questions 1–15, read the text below and look carefully at each line. Some of the lines are correct, and some have a word which should not be there. If a line is correct, put a tick (✓). If a line has a word which should not be there, write the word.

Brain training

be ______ 0 Do you remember how at school certain subjects seemed be impossible
✓ ______ 00 to understand? However much the teacher tried to explain geography,
______ 1 for example, you still did not grasp even though the basics? Now some
______ 2 psychologists are suggesting that learning difficulties may lie in the way
______ 3 the subjects are been presented rather than being a failure on the part
______ 4 of the children. According to a method that called NLP (don't worry what
______ 5 the letters stand for now), people fall into groups depending on how they
______ 6 do learn best – through sight, sound or feeling. For example, a visual
______ 7 child will to learn best through diagrams, an auditory child through spoken
______ 8 words, while a kinesthetic child will benefit most from and practical
______ 9 examples. It is easy to find out at which group your child belongs to.
______ 10 All you have to do is ask him or her a question, such as 'What was your
______ 11 day at school like?' According to the new theory of NLP, the way the child
______ 12 will answers will tell you whether they learn through sight, sound or feeling.
______ 13 So, a visual child, when answering, will look up to your right, whereas
______ 14 an auditory child will look from left to right. A child that has learns best
______ 15 through feeling will look down to the left and right before giving an answer.

Exam practice: Use of English, Part 5

3 For questions 1–10, read the text below. Use the word given in capitals at the end of each line to form a word that fits in the space in the same line.

Seven-year-olds fail test

A study by the National Foundation for (0) *Educational* Research — EDUCATION
of 3 400 seven-year-old pupils shows an (1) ______________ of basic — IGNORE
maths and English which is simply (2) ______________ . — BELIEVE
The results, which were published recently, show that one in
seven children lack basic (3) ______________ of maths and — KNOW
cannot even do simple multiplication, such as 5 x 5. The results also
show that a (4) ______________ of the children in this age group — THREE
cannot count up to 100 and do not know what (5) ______________ , — EXPRESS
such as *half* and *a quarter*, refer to. Moreover, only half of the
children had any (6) ______________ of the decimal system for money — UNDERSTAND
and only one in thirty could (7) ______________ read the temperature — ACCURACY
on a thermometer. Finally, only one in seven could say what the cost of
three 50p (8) ______________ is. — LOAF
As regards English, more than a quarter have not learnt to read
with any (9) ______________ and have problems with the alphabet; — CONFIDE
meanwhile another 25% are (10) ______________ to spell easy words, — ABLE
like *can*, *man* and *hot*.

Future (1): future simple, *going to*, present continuous, present simple

Exam practice: Use of English, Part 3

4 For questions 1–10, complete the second sentence so that it has a similar meaning to the first sentence, using the word given. Do not change the word given. You must use between two and five words, including the word given.

0 My sister is not old enough to ride a bicycle.
too
My sister is ______ *too young to* ______ ride a bicycle.

1 They intend to travel round the world when they retire.
go
They are ______________________ a world tour when they retire.

2 The weather forecast predicts a drop in temperature tomorrow.
will
They say tomorrow ______________________ colder.

3 I can't come at eleven on Saturday, as I have an appointment with the hairdresser.
having
I can't come at eleven on Saturday because ______________________ hair cut.

4 The time of departure for your flight to Rio is six o'clock
takes
The plane to Rio ______________________ six o'clock.

5 It looks like that old bridge is ready to fall down.
is
It looks like that old bridge ______________________ collapse.

6 Waiter, bring us a bottle of champagne, please.
have
Waiter, we ______________________ a bottle of champagne, please.

7 I don't mind laying the table if you do the washing up.
will
I ______________________ if you agree to wash up.

8 Have you got any plans for this evening?
doing
Are ______________________ this evening?

9 Kick off is at three o'clock sharp.
match
The ______________________ three o'clock exactly.

10 Who's your baby-sitter for this evening?
looking
Who ______________________ your baby this evening?

5 Choose the correct future form in these sentences.

1 Do you want to come to London with me on Saturday?
Thanks, but I'll go/I'm going to a football match on Saturday.
2 Where do you think you're going?
I'm leaving/I leave because I have a French lesson now.
3 What do you intend to do with yourself when you finish school?
I've decided I will/I'm going to be an actor.
4 Although the test is starting/starts at nine o'clock, you should get here fifteen minutes early.
5 Bye then. See you tonight.
Yes. I'll/I'm seeing you outside the pub at eight.
6 You're breaking/You're going to break that vase if you don't put it down.
7 OK, I'll lend/I lend you the money, but you must pay it back next week.

Questions and answers

6 Match the questions in list A with their answers in list B.

A

1 What's your teacher like?
2 What does your mum look like?
3 Whereabouts do you live?
4 What do you like to do in your spare time?
5 What are your plans for the future?
6 How do you find studying English?
7 Which famous person would you most like to meet and why?
8 What kind of music do you like?

B

a The President of the USA because he's so powerful.
b I don't have much, but I'm quite keen on tennis.
c She's tall and dark.
d Not too bad. If you get a chance to practise speaking.
e It depends on my mood – sometimes classical, sometimes techno!
f Sometimes she shouts, but usually she's OK.
g I quite fancy having my own shop.
h Not far from here.

7 Now write your own answers to the questions above.

1 ______________________________
2 ______________________________
3 ______________________________
4 ______________________________
5 ______________________________
6 ______________________________
7 ______________________________
8 ______________________________

VOCABULARY

Word formation

1 Complete this table.

verb	noun	verb	noun
arrive		examine	
believe		exist	
celebrate		inform	
conclude		invent	
decide		invite	
depart		know	
describe		predict	
dominate		promote	
enquire		publish	

2 Complete the second sentence so that it has a similar meaning to the first sentence. Use one of the nouns from the table above in each sentence.

1 I know very little about computers.
My ______________________________ poor.

2 What time does the train leave?
When ______________________________ train?

3 When he gets there, there will be someone there to meet him.
On ______________________________ him.

4 We must tell the police immediately.
We must give ______________________________ immediately.

5 When is his next book coming out?
When ______________________________ next book?

6 What did the robber look like?
Can you give me ______________________________ robber?

7 I haven't been invited to the party.
I haven't ______________________________ to the party.

8 I believe Bell invented the telephone.
The telephone ______________________________ , wasn't it?

Phrasal verbs

3 Match the phrasal verbs in list A with their meanings in list B. Two of the phrasal verbs have more than one meaning.

A	B
1 take back	a start liking someone
2 look up to	b offer someone a job
3 give up	c challenge
4 go up	d accept
5 pick up	e start an activity
6 take to	f return
7 take up	g stop an activity
8 take on	h collect
	i respect
	j increase

4 Complete these sentences using the correct form of one of the phrasal verbs above in each space. Use two of the phrasal verbs twice.

1 I ______________________ Mary the first time I saw her.
2 Your application was successful. We'll ____________ you ____________ .
3 Frazer is going to ______________________ the champion to try and win the title.
4 I would like to ______________________ your offer of a job.
5 I need to ______________________ a sport to lose some weight.
6 This milk has gone off. Let's _______ it _______ to the shop.
7 I am going to ______________________ eating meat and only eat vegetables from now on.
8 Who ______________________ the kids from school?
9 He ______________________ his teacher and takes his advice whenever he has problems.
10 The child's temperature has ______________________ . Could you call the doctor?

16 Good luck, bad luck

GRAMMAR AND USE OF ENGLISH

Exam practice: Use of English, Part 2

1 For questions 1–15, read the text below and think of the word which best fits each space. Use only one word in each space.

Happy New Year!

One of the most important days of the year is the first of January and it is celebrated (0) ___all___ over the world. It is the time of year (1) ________ people get together and eat and drink a lot and generally behave with warmth and affection (2) ________ each other. In London, on the stroke (3) ________ midnight before the New Year begins, people gather in Trafalgar Square and not (4) ________ celebrate in (5) ________ usual way but also sometimes throw themselves into the fountain under Nelson's column. In Spain, people eat (6) ________ grape for each of the twelve strokes of midnight. No one knows exactly (7) ________ the custom of celebrating the New Year began. Some people believe (8) ________ was the Chinese who started it, (9) ________ say it was the Romans. In China, they celebrate New Year, which is (10) ________ a different time from that in the West, (11) ________ only for one day but for several days. A special custom in some countries is (12) ________ make so-called 'New Year's resolutions'. This means you make a big decision to improve your life in (13) ________ way by stopping any bad habits you may (14) ________ . For example, people say they will stop smoking, they will work harder, they will do (15) ________ best to pass their exams, and so on. It is pity that the optimistic spirit of New Year often does not last very long!

Exam practice: Use of English, Part 5

2 For questions 1–10, read the text below. Use the word given in capitals at the end of each line to form a word that fits in the space in the same line.

Science or superstition?

It is difficult to come up with a reliable (0) ___definition___ of the word DEFINE
superstition, but basically it is a (1) ________ in something that BELIEVE
is not true. We all believe in some things for which we have no
(2) ________ – but can these beliefs be referred to as PROVE
superstitions? Throughout history, human (3) ________ have BE
accepted theories which turned out to be false, but the people who
believed them were sometimes not (4) ________ at all. In all periods SUPERSTITION
of history, people have had to find (5) ________ for things with EXPLAIN
the (6) ________ they have had and so beliefs that we today find KNOW

crazy seemed quite (7) ________________ at the time. For example, the famous and very (8) ________________ scientist Aristotle thought that the world was flat and for many centuries (9) ________________ on long voyages were (10) ________________ about falling off the edge of the world.

REASON
INFLUENCE
TRAVEL
ANXIETY

Conditionals (1): zero, first and second

Exam practice: Use of English, Part 3

3 For questions 1–10, complete the second sentence so that it has a similar meaning to the first sentence, using the word given. Do not change the word given. You must use between two and five words, including the word given.

0 My sister is not old enough to ride a bicycle.
too
My sister is ____*too young to*____ ride a bicycle.

1 On rainy days we don't go out.
stay
When ________________ home.

2 You should not answer any of the police's questions.
refuse
If the police ask you questions, ________________ them.

3 I won't buy a new suit unless I get a pay rise.
if
I will only ________________ I get a pay rise.

4 I would welcome a change of job.
could
If ________________ change my job.

5 A change of job would do you good.
were
If I ________________ change jobs.

6 All you have to do to switch the light on is press this button.
comes
If you press ________________ on.

7 You should ignore strangers asking for money.
ignore
If strangers ask ________________ them.

8 Going on holiday is the best way to relax.
want
If ________________ should go on holiday.

9 Don't break that vase because you'll have to pay for it.

would
If you ______________________ have to pay for it.

10 Unless I recover from my injury, I can't play on Saturday.
get
If my injury ______________________ I won't be able to play on Saturday.

4 Match the clauses in list A with the clauses in list B to make complete sentences.

A	B
1 If the taxman calls,	a I'd put on a funny face.
2 If you play with fire,	b you'll fail the exam.
3 If you don't work harder,	c leave the building immediately.
4 If I wanted to make someone laugh,	d you get fat.
5 If I saw someone cheating in an exam,	e you won't be able to drive.
6 If you sit down all the time,	f tell him I'm not here.
7 If you drink any more,	g I'd tell the teacher.
8 If you mix blue and yellow,	h I wouldn't use the lift.
9 If you hear the alarm,	i you get burnt.
10 If the building caught fire,	j you get green.

5 What advice would you give for these problems? Finish the sentences below using an appropriate conditional.

1 Your friend keeps arriving late at work after staying up all night at parties.
  a If you don't stop turning up late, *you will lose your job.*
  b If I were you, ______________________
  c If the boss asks you where you were, ______________________

2 Your friend keeps quarrelling with his/her parents because they disapprove of his/her friends.
  a If you invite your friends home, ______________________
  b If I were you, ______________________
  c If they keep bothering you, ______________________

3 Water seems to be becoming more and more scarce every year.
  a When you wash your car, ______________________
  b If we didn't leave the taps running all the time, ______________________
  c If you have a garden, ______________________

4 A friend is not sure how to spend the summer holidays.
  a If you go to Rome, ______________________
  b If you went to Paris, ______________________
  c If you go to Athens, ______________________

5 Your friend has acquired a lot of money.
  a If you tell all your friends, ______________________
  b If I were you, ______________________
  c If you get lots of begging letters, ______________________

VOCABULARY

Numbers

1 Write these figures in words.

number	words	number	words
12		250 000	
12th		2 000 000	
13th		8 August 1951	
22nd		1 May	
½		30/9/98	
¼		100%	
75th		25 × 25 =	
¾		150 ÷ 5 =	
610		34 – 6 =	

2 Complete these idioms with an appropriate word.

1 ________________ come, first served.
2 He arrived at the ________________ hour, just when everyone thought he wasn't going to turn up.
3 On ________________ thoughts, I think I will come for a curry with you.
4 ________________ time lucky.
5 ________________ a loaf is better than none.
6 Two is company, ________________ is a crowd.
7 Don't put all your eggs in ________________ basket.
8 Politicians are often ________________ - faced; you just can't trust them.

Words often confused

3 Complete these sentences using the correct form of one of the words below in each space.

destroy sprain damage crash harm demolish crack break hurt injure smash

1 I don't want to ________________ your feelings but this painting is not very good, is it?
2 A bit of hard work never did anyone any ________________ .
3 If you _______ the glasses, you will have to pay for the ________________ .
4 The car ________________ into a tree.
5 The thieves ________________ the window by throwing a brick through it.
6 The bombs ________________ the town completely.
7 They're going to ________________ that old building and put up a new one.
8 Our best player was ________________ in Saturday's match and can't play for a while.

9 I haven't broken any bones, but I think I've ________________ my ankle.

10 There's a ________________ in the window pane; I can just about see it.

Expressions and phrasal verbs with *make, do, go* and *have*

4 Put the words and phrases below into groups according to which verb they go with. Some of the words and phrases can go with more than one verb.

a baby	the beds	swimming	a swim	a try	an attempt	a go	a cake
the washing up	housework	friends	war	for a walk	skiing	nothing	a lot of work
shopping	the shopping	dinner	well	your best	a decision	money	on holiday

make ____

____

do ____

____

go ____

____

have ____

____

5 Complete these sentences using the correct form of one of the phrasal verbs below in each space. Use one of the phrasal verbs twice.

go by **go ahead** **have out** **do up** **make up** **have on** **make of**

1 We decided to ________________ with our plans, though some people disagreed.
2 We're going to have the living room ________________ as it hasn't been painted for years.
3 The actress __________ herself __________ very carefully before going to the reception.
4 I've been trying to hitch a lift but not a single car has ________________ yet.
5 I've been receiving some strange phone calls and I just don't know what to ________________ them all.
6 I __________ a tooth __________ yesterday.
7 I only __________ my pyjamas __________ and so I didn't want to go to the front door.
8 When did you learn to ________________ your own shoe-laces?

17 Worth a thousand words

GRAMMAR AND USE OF ENGLISH

Exam practice: Use of English, Part 1

1 For questions 1–15, read the text below and decide which answer A, B, C or D best fits each space.

Michaelangelo

Michaelangelo, one of the (0) ___D___ artists of all time, was born on 6th March 1475 in Caprese, where his father, Lodovico Buonarroti, (1) ________ as a magistrate for six months. Ludovico was not a wealthy man but he (2) ________ he was descended from an aristocratic family and he was very (3) ________ of this connection. Michaelangelo (4) ________ up in Settignano, a little mountain town just outside Florence. One of the first (5) ________ Michaelangelo must have become familiar with was the dome of the beautiful Cathedral in Florence, which dominated the city then as it (6) ________ does today. At school, Michaelangelo was (7) ________ an outstanding pupil; lessons did not (8) ________ to him at all. The only thing he wanted to do was to draw and '(9) ________ his time' as his elders probably called it, in the workshops of the (10) ________ painters and sculptors in the city. One can (11) ________ the eager boy, for whom art was the most important thing in his whole life, (12) ________ at the wonderful pictures and statues which filled the beautiful churches of Florence. His best friend while he was still a schoolboy was Francesco Granacci, who, (13) ________ six years older than Michaelangelo, seems to have (14) ________ an interest in the boy and helped him with his attempts to draw and paint. Michaelangelo's choice of profession did not (15) ________ his father at all. Only the most successful of artists in Florence stood any chance of making any money.

	A	B	C	D
0	A famous	B better	C biggest	D greatest
1	A made	B became	C served	D employed
2	A remarked	B claimed	C told	D announced
3	A proud	B pleased	C happy	D famous
4	A came	B grew	C lived	D took
5	A outlooks	B looks	C vision	D sights
6	A yet	B still	C already	D even
7	A by no means	B at least	C in any case	D in fact
8	A like	B attract	C appeal	D mean
9	A use	B wander	C lose	D waste
10	A variety	B groups	C difference	D various
11	A imagine	B describe	C think	D remember
12	A glimpsing	B gazing	C watching	D noticing
13	A in spite of	B despite	C even	D although
14	A put	B made	C taken	D given
15	A please	B thank	C like	D agree

Exam practice: Use of English, Part 4

2 For questions 1–15, read the text below and look carefully at each line. Some of the lines are correct, and some have a word which should not be there. If a line is correct, put a tick (✓). If a line has a word which should not be there, write the word.

A new hobby

been 0 I finished university several years ago and I've been got a degree in
have 00 Economics. Before that I have studied graphics and worked in an
________ 1 advertising agency for a short time. I realized very quickly that by trying
________ 2 to persuade people to buy things they did not really need was not my cup
________ 3 of tea. My university degree allowed me to get a job working for various
________ 4 charities so then I have worked for Oxfam and War on Want, which
________ 5 both campaign against hunger in the world and try to help poor countries
________ 6 stand on their own two feet. My ideal job would to be to work for an
________ 7 organisation like Greenpeace as a press officer or something like. After
________ 8 all these years, I have never lost interest in drawing and painting and I
________ 9 have done recently taken up a hobby: I attend art classes at the local
________ 10 college every Monday and Friday. They are teach us to use watercolours
________ 11 and I have already painted a couple of landscapes and still lifes. There
________ 12 are very various people on the course, mostly middle-aged like me.
________ 13 I think we're there for because we're all a bit bored with our lives and
________ 14 our jobs and want to do something other than going to the pub or
________ 15 sitting in front of the TV like as a vegetable.

Exam practice: Use of English, Part 5

3 For questions 1–10, read the text below. Use the word given in capitals at the end of each line to form a word that fits in the space in the same line.

I don't know much about art

Of all the (0) *criticisms* made of modern art, perhaps the most	CRITIC
common is that it is not found (1) ________ enough. This	REAL
(2) ________ is often expressed in different ways, but the	COMPLAIN
(3) ________ always comes down to the belief that the closer	ARGUE
art is to life, the (4) ________ it is. The more like a photograph	GOOD
a painting is, the more gifted the (5) ________ – 'It looks so real,'	ART
people say (6) ________ . This is why modern painters are	ADMIRE
often accused of being (7) ________ to paint and are sometimes	ABLE
even accused of (8) ________ the public. If we accept this way	CHEAT
of assessing art, then we would have to come to the	
(9) ________ that Madame Tussaud's – because it is full of	CONCLUDE
(10) ________ models of famous people – must contain greater	LIFE
art than the Louvre.	

Modal (1): obligation and necessity (*must, have to, need*)

Exam practice: Use of English, Part 3

4 For questions 1–10, complete the second sentence so that it has a similar meaning to the first sentence, using the word given. Do not change the word given. You must use between two and five words, including the word given.

0 My sister is not old enough to ride a bicycle.
too
My sister is ____too young to____ ride a bicycle.

1 Jeans are not allowed in the office.
must
You ____________________ in the office.

2 It is not necessary for you to wake me up in the morning.
have
You ____________________ wake me up in the morning.

3 Your clothes are a bit casual for a job interview.
need
You ____________________ clothes for a job interview.

4 Shorts and trainers were not permitted at my school.
let
They ____________________ shorts and trainers at my school.

5 I'd better get up early so I don't miss the bus.
must
I ____________________ late or I'll miss the bus.

6 We were obliged to have a cold shower every morning in the army.
had
We ____________________ a cold shower every morning in the army.

7 Do you want us to bring a bottle of wine to the party?
need
Do ____________________ a bottle of wine to the party?

8 We got to the airport two hours in advance though it wasn't necessary.
have
We ____________________ to the airport two hours in advance.

9 It is against the law to sell drugs to young people.
allowed
You ____________________ sell drugs to young people.

10 It is not necessary for you to buy the book – I'll lend you mine.
need
You ____________________ the book – I'll lend you mine.

5 Rewrite these sentences, making the positive sentences negative and the negative sentences positive.

1 You have to have talent to paint as a hobby.

____

2 You need to be talented to be a successful painter.

____

3 We had to do music at school.

____

4 You must practise a lot to play the piano well.

____

5 You don't need to have a loud voice to be an actor.

____

6 You need to be tall to be a successful actor.

____

7 Michaelangelo needed to go to art school to learn how to paint.

____

VOCABULARY

Countable and uncountable nouns

1 Complete this table and write C (for countable) on U (for uncountable).

verb	noun	C or U?	verb	noun	C or U?
advertise			invent		
grow			enjoy		
produce	1		equip		
	2		suggest		
televise			inform		
explain			behave		
consume			confide		
free			publicize		

2 Complete these sentences using one of the nouns from the table above in each space.

1 I believe young people have too much _______________ nowadays. They are allowed to do what they like.
2 You need a lot of _______________ to perform in front of a large audience.
3 After such bad _______________ I am not going to allow you back into the class unless you apologize!
4 You can find _______________ on the Internet about almost any subject under the sun.
5 What kind of _______________ do we need to go skiing?
6 When they interrupt programmes for advertisements it spoils my _______________ of the film.
7 I can give no _______________ for what I did. I just lost control, I don't know why.

3 Underline the countable nouns in the box below.

bread gold brush snow advice fun frame help happiness nature information knowledge painter progress weather exhibition work accommodation English gallery equipment furniture homework housework luggage music rubbish masterpiece traffic

4 Choose the correct word or words in these sentences.

1 Have you got any/all homework to do this evening?
2 She doesn't give us more/much homework; she only gives us most/a bit. She's a great teacher!
3 I need some/several advice. Can you help me?
4 She has a lot of/a great deal of knowledge of music.
5 I'm afraid you haven't made little/enough progress and you'll have to take the course again.
6 We only have a little/few furniture in the basement.
7 Do you have much more/many work to do?
8 Do you have many/any accommodation? We need three rooms for tonight.

Phrasal verbs

5 Match the phrasal verbs in list A with their meanings in list B.

A	B
1 look into	a be careful
2 run out	b go with someone about to set off on a journey
3 break off	c not be deceived by
4 see through	d meet unexpectedly
5 look out	e have no more left
6 run into	f reveal
7 let down	g stop working
8 see off	h investigate
9 break down	i end
10 let out	j disappoint

6 Complete these sentences using the correct form of one of the phrasal verbs above in each space.

1 She ____________ the secret ____________ ; now everyone knows.
2 I ____________ him ____________ at the airport.
3 I ____________________ an old friend the other day.
4 The police are ____________________ the crime.
5 I have ____________________ of patience with you! Please leave the room.
6 A good friend never ____________ you ____________.
7 The dishwasher has ____________________ again.
8 I ____________________ the trick.
9 Mary ____________________ her engagement to Arthur.
10 If you don't ____________________ , you'll fail your exams.

18 One small step

GRAMMAR AND USE OF ENGLISH

Exam practice: Use of English, Part 2

1 For questions 1–15, read the text below and think of the word which best fits each space. Use only one word in each space.

Yuri Gargarin

On 14th April 1961, a young Russian cosmonaut made history by becoming the first man (0) ___*to*___ be in space. Seven years later, and just two weeks before the anniversary (1) __________ his historic orbit around the Earth, he was killed (2) __________ a plane crash. This remarkable man was Yuri Gargarin. Gargarin (3) __________ born in Gzantsk in Russia and he began to train (4) __________ a pilot while he was still a student (5) __________ university. When he finally qualified as a pilot he (6) __________ made an officer of the Soviet Airforce. He became a cosmonaut in 1960. The space race (7) __________ the United States and the Soviet Union had already begun some years (8) __________ , but while the Americans were still getting ready to send (9) __________ first satellite into space, the Soviet Union sent *Sputnik 1* round the Earth. In 1961, Russia took the world by surprise again (10) __________ launching the *Vostock* rocket into space, inside (11) __________ was the first man in history to travel in space: Yuri Gargarin. (12) __________ first manned space flight lasted only 108 minutes, which is (13) __________ very long when you bear in mind that, nowadays, astronauts (14) __________ months, if not years, in space. After his death in a test flight (15) __________ the age of 34, his hometown of Gzantsk was renamed 'Gargarin' in his honour.

Exam practice: Use of English, Part 5

2 For questions 1–10, read the text below. Use the word given in capitals at the end of each line to form a word that fits in the space in the same line.

A close-up of the Moon

In the (0) ___*nineteenth*___ century and for most of the twentieth NINE
century up to the 1950s, the exploration of the Moon was carried
out by the use of (1) ______________ telescopes. This research POWER
provided (2) ______________ information about the visible side of the VALUE
Moon but it was only in October 1959 that the (3) ______________ SEE
side of the Moon was revealed to the world. Photographs taken
from the Soviet *Lunik III* (4) ______________ showed that the SPACE
(5) ______________ side of the Moon was, in fact, not very different HIDE
from the near side. The (6) ______________ landing of unmanned SUCCESS

spacecraft by the USA and the Russians in the 1960s and finally the landing of the first man on the Moon in 1969 made possible the direct (7) ________________ of the Moon's surface. The Apollo astronauts collected rocks and sent thousands of photographs back to (8) ________________ in Houston. They set up instruments which calculated the Moon's (9) ________________ and through the use of laser beams they discovered the exact (10) ________________ between the Moon and the Earth.

EXPLORE
HEAD
MEASURE
DISTANT

Future (2): future perfect simple, future perfect continuous, future continuous

Exam practice: Use of English, Part 3

3 For questions 1–10, complete the second sentence so that it has a similar meaning to the first sentence, using the word given. Do not change the word given. You must use between two and five words, including the word given.

0 My sister is not old enough to ride a bicycle.
too
My sister is ______ *too young to* ______ ride a bicycle.

1 This time next week, we'll be on the beach in Majorca.
lying
This time next week ________________________________ on the beach in Majorca.

2 This is my twentieth year working in this office.
working
By the end of this year, I ________________________________ in this office for twenty years.

3 6th May is our first wedding anniversary.
married
On 6th May ________________________________ for one year.

4 There's a test for all classes tomorrow morning.
doing
All the pupils ________________________________ tomorrow morning.

5 I'm going to finish writing my third letter by Friday.
written
By Friday ________________________________ my third letter.

6 If you don't need your bike tomorrow, can I borrow it?
using
If you ________________________________ your bike tomorrow, can I borrow it?

7 The new school will be ready by October.
built
The new school ________________________________ by October.

8 I have tickets for the theatre tomorrow so I can't come for a meal.
be
I can't come for a meal tomorrow because ________________________________ to the theatre.

9 Don't bother me because I will be busy all evening.
working
I ______________________________ so don't bother me.

10 By the year 2000 there will be no trees left in this town.
cut
By the year 2000 they ______________________________ all the trees in this town.

4 Complete this dialogue using the correct form (future perfect simple, future perfect continuous or future continuous) of the verbs in brackets.

Andrew: This time next week, I (1) *will be getting* (get) ready to go to the airport.
Julia: Oh, you lucky thing! Where (2) __________ you __________ (go) this time?
Andrew: I don't know what you're getting at. What do you mean, where (3) __________ I __________ (go) this time?
Julia: Well, you're always flying off somewhere.
Andrew: Rubbish! After this next trip to Oxford I (4) ____________________ (be) abroad twice this year. In fact, altogether, I (5) ____________________ (go) on four trips, two abroad and two here.
Julia: Anyway, best of luck to you. I (6) ____________________ (sit) here working hard, while you're strolling around Oxford.
Andrew: I'll have you know I (7) ____________________ (not/stroll) round Oxford. I (8) ____________________ (carry) out some very important research.
Julia: Oh, yeah, in the pubs of Oxford. By the time you come back, I (9) ____________________ (write) hundreds of letters.
Andrew: Oh, don't exaggerate, Julia. By the time I come back, you (10) ____________________ (type) just a few letters for the boss.
Julia: A few letters? I (11) ____________________ (sweat) over this word processor and making who knows how many cups of tea and coffee.
Andrew: Listen to her! Sweating over a hot word processor! Look, Julia, while you're drinking coffee every day, I (12) ____________________ (travel) hundreds of miles and when I finally get back, I (13) ____________________ (interview) dozens of people for my wretched report.
Julia: Alright, alright. When (14) __________ you __________ (leave)?
Andrew: I (15) ____________________ (catch) the British Airways flight on Wednesday morning.

5 Complete these sentences using the correct form (future perfect simple or future continuous) of the verbs in brackets.

1 By this time next year, prices in the shops *will have increased* (increase) by 30%.
2 By 2090, everyone ____________________ (speak) Chinese.
3 In ten years' time, the population of the world ____________________ (grow) to 500 million.
4 In five years' time, they ____________________ (find) a cure for cancer.
5 In twenty years' time, computers ____________________ (replace) books.
6 By 2010, people ____________________ (give up) smoking completely.
7 In five years' time, everyone ____________________ (receive) letters by E-mail.
8 In fifty years' time, everyone ____________________ (fly) in their own helicopters.
9 By the year 2020, most of us ____________________ (stop) eating beef.
10 By 2100, people ____________________ (go) on holiday to different planets.

VOCABULARY

Word formation

1 Complete this table.

verb	noun	verb	noun
accommodate		imagine	
assist		introduce	
believe		investigate	
choose		populate	
combine		publish	
complete		receive	
conclude		register	
connect		relate	1
correct			2
declare		revolve	
differ		save	
explain		speak	
express		suggest	

2 Match these definitions with nouns from the table above.

1 when you put two or more different things together = ________________
2 when you tell someone your name and a few things about yourself in a hotel = ________________
3 the number of people in a country or town = ________________
4 a word or a phrase, a way of saying something = ________________
5 somewhere to live or just stay for the night = ________________
6 A member of your family = ________________ / ________________
7 the amount of money you have in your account = ________________
8 In a school, office or hotel this is where you go first. = ________________
9 If you make mistakes, you will need some of this. = ________________
10 If things are not the same, there is one of these between them. = ________________

3 Solve the clues below to complete the crossword and to find the missing word.

1 This person gives people jobs.
2 It is useful to know this person if you want to be a famous author.
3 The boss of a school or a company.
4 This person is always going places.

5 This person travels in space.
6 This person is in charge of the office.
7 This person discovers new places.
8 It is impossible to make a film without this man.
9 This person mends your leaking pipes.
10 This person works in a hotel or a restaurant.
11 This person decides whether you are guilty or not.
12 Newspapers are full of what this person writes.
13 The missing word is ________________ .

Expressions and phrasal verbs with *get* (1)

4 Match the expressions in list A with their meanings in list B.

A	B
1 get a new car	a understand
2 get a letter	b move
3 get old/cold	c catch
4 get onto a bus or a train	d reach
5 get the table through the window	e ask, persuade
6 get the car started	f receive
7 get dinner ready	g become
8 get a cold	h cause something to happen
9 get a joke	i prepare
10 get someone to help	j buy
11 get home	k enter

5 Complete these sentences using the correct form of one of the phrasal verbs below in each space.

get away   get along   get around   get across   get at   get round to   get ahead   get off

1 I don't ____________________ much nowadays, I'm too old.
2 He's a good communicator; he knows how to ___________ his message ___________ .
3 She's really going to ____________________ with the talent she's got.
4 I ____________________ just fine with my boss; she's very friendly.
5 I was busy but I finally ____________________ writing her a letter.
6 She put the medicine on a high shelf, where the children couldn't ____________________ it.
7 I won't be able to ____________________ from work before four, so wait for me.
8 I ____________________ the bus at Oxford Street when I go shopping.

19 From rags to riches

GRAMMAR AND USE OF ENGLISH

Exam practice: Use of English, Part 1

1 For questions 1–15, read the text below and decide which answer A, B, C or D best fits each space.

A new life

It took a few days after the cheque had arrived for me to (0) ___B___ that our life would never be the same again – it was a dream (1) ________ true. Like everyone else, I had often (2) ________ what it would be like not having to worry about paying the bills and just (3) ________ ends meet. My husband, Colin, always (4) ________ to say there would come a day when we could (5) ________ the lights on without worrying how much it was going to (6) ________ us. Colin had been out of work for the last (7) ________ of years and we had begun to wonder whether things would (8) ________ get better. He had become depressed and irritable. Suddenly, we were (9) ________ plans to move into a big, new house in one of the more fashionable suburbs of town. We knew that we would lose (10) ________ with the neighbours with whom we had shared so much (11) ________ the years, but both of us felt we needed more space and a proper garden. I had always been (12) ________ on gardening but there hadn't been much scope for my talents in the little (13) ________ of grass we had at the front and the tiny (14) ________ at the back of the house. Before moving, however, we decided to (15) ________ ourselves to a nice, long holiday.

	A	B	C	D
0	A notice	B realize	C find	D convince
1	A made	B come	C being	D become
2	A planned	B predicted	C imagined	D enjoyed
3	A having	B doing	C putting	D making
4	A would	B had	C used	D repeated
5	A let	B leave	C remember	D see
6	A cost	B pay	C spend	D ask
7	A dozen	B few	C several	D couple
8	A hardly	B sometimes	C ever	D rather
9	A making	B drawing	C looking	D having
10	A time	B communication	C touch	D friendship
11	A in	B over	C at	D for
12	A fond	B good	C enthusiastic	D keen
13	A part	B patch	C piece	D blades
14	A court	B square	C entrance	D yard
15	A treat	B enjoy	C give	D spoil

Exam practice: Use of English, Part 4

2 For questions 1–15, read the text below and look carefully at each line. Some of the lines are correct, and some have a word which should not be there. If a line is correct, put a tick (✓). If a line has a word which should not be there, write the word.

Journey of my dreams

___✓___ 0 Until a few months ago, Colin, my husband, was looking for a job without
___*big*___ 00 big success and feeling life had little to offer to him. Now, after winning the
________ 1 Lottery, we are rich and are both in a position to enjoy our leisure time as we
________ 2 have never been able to do in our lives before. Our children are being grown
________ 3 up and living abroad so we have no one to share out our good fortune with.
________ 4 Anyway, we have decided to go on a long cruise. Colin came home a few
________ 5 days ago with a huge pile of some colourful brochures for exotic holidays, the
________ 6 kind of holiday I thought only film stars went on, not people like us. Now it
________ 7 will be me lying on the deck of a luxury liner, sipping my Campari and sunbathing
________ 8 as we will sail to some far-off destination. The idea of a swimming pool on a ship
________ 9 is something more I have only read about. We started looking through the
________ 10 brochures last night, for finding all those mythical places very tempting. It is hard to
________ 11 believe that the Pyramids and the Taj Mahal will not just still be pictures in a book,
________ 12 but that we could actually be there, standing inside and having our photograph
________ 13 taken so we can show people back in home that we have really been. Of course
________ 14 we will have to buy a new camera; our little Kodak hasn't been working good
________ 15 since our Harry's wedding, which was ten whole years ago. And when I think of
the washing machine we couldn't afford to get repaired six months ago ...

Exam practice: Use of English, Part 5

3 For questions 1–10, read the text below. Use the word given in capitals at the end of each line to form a word that fits in the space in the same line.

Just a bit of fun?

For many people, playing card games is one of the most
(0) ___*enjoyable*___ ways of spending their leisure time. Indeed, in ENJOY
some cultures card games and even an element of (1) ________________ GAMBLE
amongst friends and family is quite common on certain special
occasions, such as New Year's Eve. (2) ________________ at cards is WIN
a bit like having your fortune told – it is a (3) ________________ bit of fun. HARM
Even if you don't win, you can take comfort in sayings, such as
'(4) ________________ at cards, lucky in love.' It is often LUCK
(5) ________________ to watch someone who has never played cards AMUSE
before beat all the experts. This is called '(6) ________________ luck' BEGIN
and it adds to the fun. Some people find it (7) ________________ just FASCINATE
watching a game of cards, while others find the whole thing
incredibly (8) ________________ if they are not taking an active part. BORE
(9) ________________ , for some people card games become an FORTUNATE
(10) ________________ that they cannot control. ADDICT

Conditionals (2): third and mixed

Exam practice: Use of English, Part 3

4 For questions 1–10, complete the second sentence so that it has a similar meaning to the first sentence, using the word given. Do not change the word given. You must use between two and five words, including the word given.

0 My sister is not old enough to ride a bicycle.
too
My sister is ______ *too young to* ______ ride a bicycle.

1 She didn't go to the party and had an awful evening.
nice
If she had gone to the party, she ______ evening.

2 It's too hot to go for a walk today.
if
We could go for a walk ______ hot today.

3 I managed to get up on time by going to bed early.
late
If I ______ I wouldn't have got up on time.

4 If you buy a ticket, you will win some money.
any
You ______ if you don't buy a ticket.

5 The accident happened because you were driving so fast.
driving
If you had ______ the accident wouldn't have happened.

6 I would like you to give me a ring the moment you arrive.
please
As soon as ______ me a ring.

7 She was upset because I forgot her birthday.
been
She ______ happier if I hadn't forgotten her birthday.

8 I didn't pass the exam so I am taking it again.
would
If I had passed the exam, I ______ it again.

9 Take my advice and marry when you are older.
get
If I were you, ______ later.

10 He went on a diet and lost a lot of weight.
so
If he hadn't gone on a diet, he would ______ weight.

Modals (2): certainty and speculation (*must, may, might, could, can't*)

5 Match the sentences in list A with the appropriate responses in list B.

A

1 He is wearing a ring.
2 He is tall and very athletic.
3 She refused to eat cake and ice-cream.
4 Next door they are playing music and dancing.
5 They look suntanned and very relaxed.
6 He was able to play the piano when he was five.
7 All the lights are switched off in their house.
8 She looks completely different from you.
9 He is tall, has blond hair and speaks German.
10 He has a slightly foreign accent.

B

a He might be a basketball player.
b They must have been on holiday.
c She can't be your twin sister.
d He must be a genius.
e He could be Austrian.
f He could be a married man.
g They must be having a party.
h He must have lived abroad for a few years.
i She must be on a diet.
j They must have gone to bed.

6 Read the puzzle below.

Anthony is lying dead on the floor in the bedroom. Around his body there is some broken glass and some water. The door of the room is locked. The window is open. Who is Anthony? How did he die?

Here are ten clues. Complete the clues using *can't*, *could*, *might* or *must* and the correct form of the verbs in brackets. Use the clues to solve the puzzle.

1 There is only a little water, so Anthony ______________________ (drown).
2 There's no blood, so Anthony ______________________ (stab).
3 There is no gun either, so he ______________________ (shot).
4 Cleopatra also lives in the house but she was asleep in the room next door, so she ______________________ (kill) Anthony.
5 He ______________________ (have) a heart attack. (But he didn't!)
6 The glass is not from a drinking glass.
7 Cleopatra was very fond of Anthony, so she ______________________ (kill) him.
8 Anthony ______________________ (commit) suicide then! (No, he didn't!)
9 Someone ______________________ (poison) him! (No, he wasn't poisoned!)
10 Cleopatra owns a cat called Caesar.

Answer: Anthony is a ____________________ and he must have died

____

Answer: Anthony is a goldfish. Caesar the cat came through the open window and tried to get Anthony out of the goldfish bowl with his paw. The bowl fell off the table and smashed on the floor. The cat leapt out of the window because of the noise, leaving Anthony to die on the floor from suffocation.

VOCABULARY

Shops and services

1 Solve the clues below to complete the crossword and to find the missing word.

1 Can we go to the bank? I need to _______________ some money.
2 Is this a spy who sells newspapers?
3 The opposite of cheap is _______________ .
4 You wait here for the train.
5 If you want to make sure the letter gets there, send it by _______________ post.
6 This where you have your money in a bank.
7 This person sells fish.
8 This is where you pay in a supermarket.
9 This does not mean it isn't valuable but that it is very valuable.
10 How much does that dress _______________ ?
11 The American word for shop is _______________ .
12 This person does not work with trains but sells paper.
13 A big shop or house has many of these.
14 You carry your luggage or shopping in one of these.
15 Another word for expensive is _______________ .
16 The missing word is _______________ .

Word formation

2 Match words from list A with words from list B to make compound nouns. Use some of the words more than once.

A	B	
shop	money	*shop assistant*
department	hostel	_______________
news	card	_______________
post	assistant	_______________
youth	goods	_______________
travel	office	_______________
credit	food	_______________
shoe	store	_______________
luxury	shop	_______________
junk	agent	_______________
pocket		_______________

3 Complete these sentences using one of the compound nouns from exercise 2 in each space.

1 I wonder how much those shoes are? Let's ask the ________________ .
2 Where shall we go for our holiday? Let's go to a ________________ .
3 The hotels are full. Why don't we stay in the ________________ ?
4 If you want to buy lots of different things, you should go to a ________________ .
5 I want to pick up a registered letter so I have to go the ________________ .
6 The government has put a high tax on ________________ .
7 Children often complain that their parents don't give them enough ________________ .

Phrasal verbs with *get* (2)

4 Match the phrasal verbs in list A with their meanings in list B. Two of the phrasal verbs have two meanings.

A	B
1 get down	a manage, survive
2 get over	b write down
3 get by	c become known
4 get through	d persuade
5 get round	e succeed (in an exam)
6 get off	f depress
7 get ahead	g leave (a bus)
8 get down to	h start
	i be successful
	j recover

5 Complete these sentences using the correct form of one of the phrasal verbs above in each space.

1 If you want to ____________________ , you have to have talent but also a lot of luck.
2 Once the news had ____________________ that they were getting married, the telephone wouldn't stop ringing.
3 Don't speak so fast because I can't ____________________ all the information.
4 She did very well in physics, but I'm afraid she failed to ____________________ the maths paper.
5 To get to the museum, ____________________ the bus at Trafalgar Square and then walk up the first street on your right.
6 She's just had an operation but she's beginning to ____________________ it now.
7 Thinking about all the hungry people in the world really __________ me __________ .
8 My mum didn't want me to go to the party at first but in the end I managed to ____________________ her and she let me go.
9 OK, the break's over now, let's ____________________ some work.
10 We're not rich but we make ends meet. We just about ____________________ .

20 An American dream

GRAMMAR AND USE OF ENGLISH

Exam practice: Use of English, Part 2

1 For questions 1–15, read the text below and think of the word which best fits each space. Use only one word in each space.

A world language

The English language is big business: every day more and (0) ___*more*___ people around the world are learning English (1) ___________ a foreign language and more and more people (2) ___________ making a living from providing English in various forms, including teachers, writers and publishers. (3) ___________ Britain, the English language is one of the country's (4) ___________ important sources of income.

English is quite unique in the history (5) ___________ the world's languages: an amazing one in seven people in the world speak (6) ___________ , which makes it undoubtedly the first world language in history. (7) ___________ English, Latin, French and Greek were also to some extent international languages (8) ___________ none of them ever managed to reach either the number of users that English has (9) ___________ the incredible range of situations in (10) ___________ English is used today. For example, 75% of the world's correspondence and 60% of the world's telephone conversations are carried (11) ___________ in English. Chinese also has a billion speakers, but (12) ___________ a Chinese businessman meets a Spanish colleague at a conference, they (13) ___________ almost certainly use English as the medium of communication, (14) ___________ Chinese or Spanish. English has also become the language of science: two thirds of scientists write (15) ___________ research papers in English and the majority of doctors in the world learn English as part of their studies.

Exam practice: Use of English, Part 4

2 For questions 1–15, read the text below and look carefully at each line. Some of the lines are correct, and some have a word which should not be there. If a line is correct, put a tick (✓). If a line has a word which should not be there, write the word.

Looking for a job

___*being*___ 0 This year I celebrate twenty years as being an English teacher. I am often
___✓___ 00 asked how I chose this career. In fact, I didn't choose it: I drifted into it,
________ 1 like a lot of such other people who have become English teachers. When I
________ 2 finished university what I have really wanted to do was act – the theatre was,
________ 3 and still is, my first love. I tried to get it into drama school and nearly managed
________ 4 it. I don't think my acting was the problem. In one drama school it was my
________ 5 singing one; the director said a successful actor needs to be able to both sing
________ 6 and dance. I have never been very good at either. He sat at the piano while I
________ 7 tried to sing a much well-known tune – I was not Pavarotti. At another school,

________ 8 I was foolish enough to admit I didn't have any money with which to pay up the
________ 9 fees for my training, so even if though they thought I could act, they couldn't
________ 10 see how I was going to pay my way. I had reached a dead end. Then I saw
________ 11 a poster in the university English department which advertising jobs for teachers
________ 12 in Italy. I had always wanted to go to Italy because I had heard of so much about
________ 13 it from my father. He had been born in Italy and ran a small pizzeria in Camden
________ 14 Town. Just for fun a friend and I we decided to go along to the interview in
________ 15 London, though we had not been inside a classroom since we left school.

Exam practice: Use of English, Part 5

3 For questions 1–10, read the text below. Use the word given in capitals at the end of each line to form a word that fits in the space in the same line.

Hollywood forever?

Apart from television, the cinema is the most popular form of	
(0) *entertainment* for most people because it is still relatively	ENTERTAIN
(1) ____________ . Hollywood is, of course, the capital of the	EXPENSE
(2) ____________ cinema industry. Hollywood movies make up	NATION
(3) ____________ 75% of all the films we watch at our local cinemas.	ROUGH
Although we may find it difficult to remember the names of	
(4) ____________ and French film stars, Hollywood stars, such as	ITALY
Sylvester Stallone and Meryl Streep are (5) ____________ names	HOUSE
all around the world. Moreover, only Hollywood seems to make	
certain kinds of films (6) ____________ .	SUCCESS
(7) ____________ are one example but we can also include westerns,	MUSIC
although for a time 'spaghetti westerns' (made in Italy) were quite	
(8) ____________ with cinema goers. But cowboys and Indians are	FASHION
really a Hollywood (9) ____________ and they are still going strong	SPECIAL
after all these years. Such films, however, have not remained	
(10) ____________ by time and changes in attitudes. The cowboys	TOUCH
are no longer always the goodies as they were in the 1940s.	

Verbs followed by infinitive with or without *to*

Exam practice: Use of English, Part 3

4 For questions 1–10, complete the second sentence so that it has a similar meaning to the first sentence, using the word given. Do not change the word given. You must use between two and five words, including the word given.

0 My sister is not old enough to ride a bicycle.
too
My sister is *too young to* ride a bicycle.

1 I suppose you are very tired after your long walk.
must
You ______________________________ after your long walk.

2 'I won't come home late from the party,' she said.
promised
She ______________________________ late from the party.

3 It would have been better if you had gone to bed earlier.
should
You ______________________________ to bed so late.

4 We were allowed to stay up late if there was a good film on television.
let
My parents ______________________________ if there was a good film on television.

5 'Don't swim just after you have eaten,' she said to them.
warned
She ______________________________ swim just after they had eaten.

6 We had to do a lot of homework at my school.
made
We ______________________________ a lot of homework at my school.

7 I prefer reading books to playing with computers.
rather
I'd ______________________________ play with computers.

8 The sound of birds singing in the trees makes me feel good.
hear
I feel good ______________________________ in the trees.

9 The general gave the order to fire on the enemy to the soldiers.
ordered
The ______________________________ fire on the enemy.

10 I'm sure there was an insect crawling up my back just now.
felt
I'm sure ______________________________ up my back just now.

5 Complete this letter using the correct form (with or without *to*) of one of the verbs below in each space.

visit ask be begin recommend do have hear get stay book go tell hire check

Dear Jenny,

Thanks for your letter. I'm pleased (1) ______________ you're going to the States this year and I would (2) ______________ delighted to give you some tips to make your trip as enjoyable as possible.

Let me (3) ______________ you first of all that you won't need (4) ______________ a visa and you are allowed (5) ______________ for up to three months. I am not sure about the details, so you'd better (6) ______________ with your local American consulate.

I started my visit in New York, but you may prefer (7) ______________ on the West Coast (California) and then travel eastwards. If you can afford (8) ______________ so, I would advise you (9) ______________ a car, but otherwise you can (10) ______________ around very comfortably on the Greyhound buses. If you would like (11) ______________ Hollywood, you'll have (12) ______________ to Los Angeles, which is huge and polluted. You can (13) __________________ a place on a guided tour round some of the big studios, which I'd highly (14) __________________ . Finally, look out for some stars! When I was in LA, I saw Tom Cruise in a restaurant. I wanted (15) __________________ for his autograph but he was gone before I could get my notebook out.

I hope that what I've written will be of some help. Have a wonderful time and send me a postcard!

Yours,
Maria

Gerunds (-*ing* forms)

6 Complete these sentences using the -*ing* form of one of the verbs below in each space.

hear complain lend have meet walk lie cook play laugh

1 I enjoy __________________ on the beach and doing nothing all day.
2 I hate __________________ people my books and having to ask for them back months later.
3 I can't stand __________________ in the rain without an umbrella.
4 I can't help __________________ when people trip over.
5 __________________ for other people is my favourite way of relaxing.
6 It's no use __________________ about something you can't change.
7 I can see some children __________________ outside my window.
8 I am just not interested in __________________ all about your summer holidays.
9 I am anxious about __________________ to go into hospital.
10 I remember __________________ you for the first time – it was five years ago.

VOCABULARY

Homonyms

1 Homonyms are words that are spelt and pronounced the same, but have different meanings. Complete these pairs of sentences using one of the words below for each pair.

way tap fall rock case serve spend kind train odd

1 How much do you __________________ a week?
Where are you going to __________________ your holidays?
2 It was very __________________ of you to meet me at the station.
What __________________ of music do you like?
3 I heard a light __________________ on the door.
Turn the hot __________________ on.
4 Whose turn is it to __________________ the ball?
You can __________________ your country in many ways.
5 If you want to be in the team, you'll have to __________________ every day.
I love travelling by __________________ .

6 Have you packed your ________________ for the trip?
A famous lawyer was handling the ________________ .

7 Careful you don't ________________ and hurt yourself.
In the ________________ the leaves turn to yellow.

8 If you can't find your ________________ , ask someone.
The best ________________ to solve the problem is to discuss it.

9 His behaviour has been rather ________________ lately.
There is an ________________ number of us, so someone can't play.

10 A huge ________________ came rolling down the mountain.
When the baby's sleepy, I take it in my arms and ________________ it.

Phrasal verbs

2 Replace the underlined words in these sentences with the correct form of one of the phrasal verbs below. Make any other changes that are necessary.

come across put forward keep up put up with cut down turn up make out put out take on put on

1 I was just walking along the street when I bumped into someone I hadn't seen for years.

____

2 It's odd how people you haven't seen for years appear unexpectedly in the strangest places.

____

3 The lessons were much too difficult for me and I found it difficult to do all the work.

____

4 At the committee meeting I suggested an idea but no one liked it.

____

5 I want to lose weight so I'm eating fewer cakes and sweets.

____

6 Some football players fall to the ground and pretend they are in pain.

____

7 I will not tolerate such behaviour – it must stop!

____

8 He threw water over the flames in an attempt to extinguish the fire.

____

9 We are going to perform a play at school this Christmas.

____

10 The director gave me a job as an English teacher.

____

21 Potato races

GRAMMAR AND USE OF ENGLISH

Exam practice: Use of English, Part 1

1 For questions 1–15, read the text below and decide which answer A, B, C or D best fits each space.

In the lion's den

I'm an Aston Villa fan and (0) __D__ I don't take much of an interest in the game generally, I (1) ________ my local team whenever they play at home and I usually turn (2) ________ for a few important matches in other cities. This time they were playing Liverpool in a vital semi-final match and I travelled all the (3) ________ to London to see it. I had had difficulty getting hold of a ticket and had only (4) ________ it at the last minute. The whole thing (5) ________ out to be a big mistake. There wasn't much choice about where to stand and, to my (6) ________ , I found myself in a part of the stadium which was (7) ________ with Liverpool fans who had already had too much to drink and the referee hadn't even (8) ________ the whistle for kick-off yet. I recognized a (9) ________ other Villa supporters in the midst of the Liverpool crowd who, unlike me, were not only wearing but (10) ________ the team's scarf so they (11) ________ out like a sore thumb against the sea of Liverpool fans. They were singing and chanting and generally (12) ________ a good time. I thought the situation might become nasty so I just (13) ________ quiet. There was a roar and more chanting from the crowd as the two teams came running onto the (14) ________ . At last, the referee blew his whistle and the big match was underway. Most of the first half was pretty dull with only a few (15) ________ at goal but then everything changed when the referee awarded our side a penalty. Of course the Liverpool fans went crazy and started throwing objects onto the field and smashing anything they could get hold of.

	A	B	C	D
0	A despite	B even	C however	D although
1	A follow	B clap	C support	D like
2	A on	B down	C away	D up
3	A way	B journey	C road	D miles
4	A reached	B managed	C arrived	D succeeded
5	A turned	B made	C found	D ended
6	A confusion	B fear	C surprise	D shock
7	A full	B squashed	C squeezed	D packed
8	A started	B blown	C played	D taken
9	A few	B crowd	C group	D number
10	A holding	B taking	C throwing	D waving
11	A stood	B made	C looked	D appeared
12	A making	B doing	C having	D enjoying
13	A continued	B made	C kept	D went
14	A pitch	B grass	C stands	D stadium
15	A tries	B kicks	C attacks	D shots

Exam practice: Use of English, Part 4

2 For questions 1–15, read the text below and look carefully at each line. Some of the lines are correct, and some have a word which should not be there. If a line is correct, put a tick (✓). If a line has a word which should not be there, write the word.

The king of sports?

___✓___ 0 The stadium is only a few minutes away from where I live so I usually
___the___ 00 go to matches on the foot. I put on my team's colours and set off with a
________ 1 couple of friends from work. I always feel a sense of excitement as I turn
________ 2 to the corner and the tall floodlights come into view at the top of the main
________ 3 stand of the stadium. By the time we will get to the stadium, there are big
________ 4 enough crowds, all heading in the same direction. As soon as we get
________ 5 inside, the chanting begins and the suspense builds up. I have been to a lot
________ 6 of games which were utterly boring: the weather was such cold and drizzly
________ 7 and the game finished in a goal-less draw. After going games like that, some
________ 8 fans express their disappointment through acts of violence but I just look ahead
________ 9 to the next game. Violence on and off of the pitch is the biggest problem in
________ 10 football, but the behaviour of some of the stars also gives the game a bad name.
________ 11 If we take Maradona of Argentina: he was, as everyone knows it, a great
________ 12 player but he got involved with drugs and was excluded from the 1994 World
________ 13 Cup after he failing a drugs test. Another of the greatest players was the
________ 14 Englishman George Best, but again the pressure of being a star was too great
________ 15 for him. He turned up to drink and retired when he was only twenty-six.

Exam practice: Use of English, Part 5

3 For questions 1–10, read the text below. Use the word given in capitals at the end of each line to form a word that fits in the space in the same line.

The Olympics: another view

(0) ___Unlike___ most people, I took no interest whatsoever in the LIKE
last Olympics because (1) ________________ I see the whole thing as a BASIC
circus: it is a circus where athletes perform tricks and it is a circus
for big business. I am sure my views are not typical of how the
(2) ________________ of sports fans feel about the Olympic Games. In my MAJOR
opinion, the commercialization of sport through (3) ________________ SPONSOR
and (4) ________________ is causing the Games serious damage. ADVERT
During the event, television is full of (5) ________________ for expensive COMMERCE
trainers, clothes and sports (6) ________________ aimed EQUIP
(7) ________________ at teenagers, whose parents can ill afford to buy PARTICULAR
them such things. What I also find (8) ________________ is the way DISAPPOINT
teams are now called after the company that sponsors them.
Finally, there is the (9) ________________ way in which gold medallists RIDICULE
become well-known (10) ________________ overnight and make a lot of PERSON
money appearing in adverts for trainers or breakfast cereal.

Describing a sequence of events

Exam practice: Use of English, Part 3

4 For questions 1–10, complete the second sentence so that it has a similar meaning to the first sentence, using the word given. Do not change the word given. You must use between two and five words, including the word given.

0 My sister is not old enough to ride a bicycle.
too
My sister is ______too young to______ ride a bicycle.

1 First I'll get a bit of sleep and then I'll get the dinner ready.
nap
After I ______________________ I'll get the dinner ready.

2 The first thing the police did when they got here was to take my fingerprints.
arrived
As ______________________ they took my fingerprints.

3 I can only start washing the dishes when you finish eating.
have
Once ______________________ I can start washing the dishes.

4 As soon as the players appeared on the pitch the crowd roared.
moment
The ______________________ on the pitch the crowd roared.

5 We went to the theatre but they had sold out of tickets.
got
By ______________________ to the theatre there were no tickets left.

6 We can't leave if John doesn't arrive.
until
We'll ______________________ arrives.

7 As soon as the lesson had finished I went home.
straight
I ______________________ the lesson.

8 Please try the plan and then make comments.
given
Don't make any comments about the plan before ______________________ try.

9 If you haven't had enough practice, don't take part in the show.
unless
Don't take part in the show ______________________ practice.

10 On my return from London I'll telephone you.
get
I'll give you a ______________________ from London.

5 Rewrite these sentences using the word or phrase in brackets.

1 Take your umbrella with you because it might rain. (in case)

____

2 You can go to the party but you must come back by midnight. (as long as)

____

3 On hearing the news she telephoned her mother. (as soon as)

____

4 It is a pity I don't know Spanish. (wish)

____

5 Read the instructions and then switch the machine on. (before)

____

6 Finish the task before you stop working. (until)

____

7 We'll have to leave now. (time)

____

8 I can't afford to buy that car yet. (when)

____

Linking and contrasting ideas

6 Complete this text using one of the words or phrases below in each space.

in addition	**as for**	**in spite of**	**what's more**	**even though**
to sum up	**firstly**	**not only ... but also**	**finally**	**however**

Making a speech

Well, here we are at the end of the conference and it's nearly time for us all to go home. Before we do, I'd like to say a few things. (1) ___Firstly___ , let me begin by thanking the chairperson of the association for organizing the conference so well, (2) ________________ various difficulties. (3) ________________ , I would like to make one suggestion: why not hold the conference over three days instead of two? (4) ________________ to allow more people to give talks, (4) ________________ to allow visitors to this beautiful city to see some of the sights? (5) ________________ , a longer conference would make it possible for participants to get to know each other better. But to get back to my words of thanks ... (6) ________________ to the chairperson, I know that we would all like to show our appreciation to the conference staff, who through their hard work have made the last few days run so smoothly. (7) ________________ , on a personal note, I would like to thank my university for giving me leave to attend the conference (8) ________________ this is one of the busiest times in the year for all of us. (9) ________________ my wife and children, there are no words to express my gratitude for their support and patience. There is little more I would like to say at this stage so, (10) ________________ , I feel the conference has been a great success and it has taught us all a great deal about ...

VOCABULARY

Homophones

1 Homophones are words that sound the same, but have different spellings and different meanings. Complete these pairs of sentences using the words below.

plane/plain	**weight/wait**	**flu/flew**	**fare/fair**	**scene/seen**
aloud/allowed	**air/heir**	**raise/rays**	**tires/tyres**	**sight/site**

1 In the first ________________ of the play the hero meets the heroine.
Children should be ________________ but not heard.

2 The ozone layer protects us from the ________________ of the sun.
It is difficult for a mother to ________________ three children on her own.

3 Can you please ________________ your turn?
What are you doing to bring down your ________________ ?

4 Prince Charles is the ________________ to the British throne.
She has an ________________ of confidence about her.

5 The accident was a terrible ________________ .
I have been working on a building ________________ .

6 I caught ________________ and was off work for a week.
She ________________ into a rage when she saw the mess on the floor.

7 She has a rather ________________ appearance but she is very charming.
The ________________ was delayed and then cancelled because of air traffic problems.

8 Cleaning the house from top to bottom really ________________ you out.
You should get new ________________ for your car; they're completely bald!

9 Are we ________________ to leave the room during the test?
Read the text ________________ so we can all hear you.

10 How much is the bus ________________ to the nearest town?
There is a huge international ________________ every year in the capital city.

Expressions with *time*

2 Complete these sentences using one of the words below in each space.

many	**from**	**table**	**pass**	**first**	**take**	**this**	**wasting**	**your**	**the**
one	**tell**	**is**	**on**	**five**	**all**	**at**	**spends**	**good**	**half**

1 ______________ your time, there's no hurry.

2 It ______________ time we were on our way.

3 ______________ time next week, we'll be on our way to Jamaica.

4 I do sport ______________ times a week.

5 How ______________ times do I have to tell you to keep quiet?

6 I remember ______________ time we used to play hide and seek.

7 Can I take up a bit of _______________ time?
8 She keeps complaining _______________ the time.
9 The _______________ time I went to the theatre was when I was about ten.
10 She _______________ her time watching TV all day.
11 We had a _______________ time at the party.
12 Stop _______________ your time. Get on with some work!
13 At _______________ time children were forced to work cleaning chimneys.
14 I see Trevor _______________ time to time. Not very often, I'm afraid.
15 _______________ times I feel like just giving up and finding another job.
16 Listening to the radio helped me to _______________ the time.
17 The score at _______________ time was three-nil.
18 Have you got a railway time - _______________ ?
19 Can you _______________ me the time?
20 She always comes __________ time to meetings.

Phrasal verbs

3 Complete these sentences using the correct form of one of the phrasal verbs below in each space.

catch on	catch up	drop out	drop off	kick off	join in	fall behind
fall out	kick out	join up	play away	play up	send off	send up

1 I am not friends with Peter anymore. We've ______________________ .
2 Don't just sit there watching the game, ______________________ !
3 If there is a war and they want soldiers for the army, would you ______________________ ?
4 I'm looking forward to the match. What time do they ______________________ ?
5 The pupil misbehaved so much that the teacher had to ____________ him ____________ .
6 She let the naughty pupil back into class as long as he stopped ______________________ .
7 After the first year I couldn't cope with university, so I decided to ______________________ .
8 That style looks so old-fashioned; I don't think clothes like that will ever ______________________ .
9 The other runners were so far ahead that it was difficult for him to ______________________ .
10 She couldn't catch up with the other runners because she had ____________ too far ____________ .
11 After the player had committed his fourth foul, the referee had to ____________ him ____________ .
12 The prime minister has got such a funny voice, it is easy to ____________ him ____________ .
13 When we got to the market I asked the taxi driver to ____________ me ____________ .
14 A game against an opposing team is more difficult when you ______________________ .

22 Holidays are bad for your health

GRAMMAR AND USE OF ENGLISH

Exam practice: Use of English, Part 2

1 For questions 1–15, read the text below and think of the word which best fits each space. Use only one word in each space.

A weekend in Tenerife

The weekend was a disaster. Have you ever (0) ___*been*___ to Tenerife? Given a choice between Siberia and a four-star hotel in Playa de las Americas, I'd choose Siberia any day. Playa de las Americas is the name of the resort (1) ___________ we stayed. Laurence chose it from the travel agent's brochures (2) ___________ it's near the airport and we were due to arrive late (3) ___________ night. Well, that seemed to make sense but it turned (4) ___________ to be the most awful place you can imagine. *Playa* is the Spanish (5) ___________ beach, but the resort doesn't have a beach, not what I'd call a beach, anyway – just a strip of black mud. (6) ___________ the beaches in Tenerife are black because the whole island is basically an enormous lump of coke and the beaches are made (7) ___________ powdered coke; it's volcanic, you see. Apparently, only a few years (8) ___________ it was just a barren shoreline and then some businessmen decided to build a resort (9) ___________ and now it's Blackpool beside the Atlantic. There's a main street (10) ___________ is always choked with traffic and lined with the most vulgar bars, cafés and discos you ever saw, with deafening music and flashing lights and greasy cooking smells all round the clock. (11) ___________ from that there's nothing except block after block of high-rise hotels and apartments. It's a concrete nightmare with (12) ___________ any trees or grass. We didn't realize how horrible (13) ___________ was immediately because it was dark (14) ___________ we arrived and the taxi from the airport took (15) ___________ by what seemed to me to be a suspiciously roundabout route.

Exam practice: Use of English, Part 4

2 For questions 1–15, read the text below and look carefully at each line. Some of the lines are correct, and some have a word which should not be there. If a line is correct, put a tick (✓). If a line has a word which should not be there, write the word.

A room with a view

___*out*___ 0 When I arrived on the island the first thing I had to do was find out
___✓___ 00 somewhere to stay. Although the harbour was crowded with hotels and
________ 1 houses who offering rooms (with hot water and panoramic views),
________ 2 I preferred to head straight for one of the small hotels recommended by
________ 3 my guide book. So that with my pack on my back, I struggled up the steep
________ 4 hill that led to the Sunview Hotel. It was a hard work and I wished I had
________ 5 taken a taxi, as although it was still only May the weather it was already
________ 6 very hot. To make things worse, the Sunview was completely booked up

_______ 7 and I had to continue my search. The owner, who was friendly and helpful,
_______ 8 told me I should have phoned earlier but he also told me that where I would
_______ 9 find a vacant room. I have followed his directions and came to a little,
_______ 10 concrete block, with a big sign saying 'Rooms' hanging from an olive tree in
_______ 11 the front yard. Luckily, they already had a couple of free rooms and I chose
_______ 12 the one with the best view. After I having a quick shower, I set out to explore
_______ 13 the town. Arriving in May meant I could to avoid the crowds, which in the
_______ 14 high season fill the narrow streets. Now I nearly had the place to myself,
_______ 15 except for a few German tourists and except elderly English couples who were
staying in the four-star hotel just outside the town.

Exam practice: Use of English, Part 5

3 For questions 1–10, read the text below. Use the word given in capitals at the end of each line to form a word that fits in the space in the same line.

Getting away from it all

How many times have you come back from what was meant to be	
a (0) ___relaxing___ holiday and said, 'If only I had stayed at home!'	RELAX
Why are holidays often more (1) ______________ than staying home?	STRESS
It is not actually very (2) ______________ that foreign travel is tiring and	SURPRISE
it is not just because of the distances involved. A (3) ______________	SUCCESS
trip needs planning and very careful (4) ______________ – this is	PREPARE
hard work. Having set off, you will probably have to spend hours	
in stuffy airports because of (5) ______________ delays.	END
(6) ______________ , as everyone knows, is itself a stressful experience	FLY
for most people. Finally, you arrive in an (7) ______________ environment	FAMILIAR
with perhaps no (8) ______________ whatsoever of the local language.	KNOW
It is almost like becoming a child again: one feels so (9) ______________	HELP
and stupid. Imagine not being able to explain what you want to eat to a	
(10) ______________ or where you are staying to a taxi driver!	WAIT

Expressing wishes and regrets; inversion

Exam practice: Use of English, Part 3

4 For questions 1–10, complete the second sentence so that it has a similar meaning to the first sentence, using the word given. Do not change the word given. You must use between two and five words, including the word given.

0 My sister is not old enough to ride a bicycle.
too
My sister is ___too young to___ ride a bicycle.

1 What a shame we didn't go to Paris instead.
gone
If ______________________________ Paris instead.

2 You didn't choose the right resort.
chosen
You ______________________________ another resort.

3 I regret not going to Mykonos when I was younger.
wish
I ______________________________ Mykonos when I was younger.

4 What a pity Tenerife was so noisy.
wish
I ______________________________ so noisy.

5 I would love to visit Seville in the Spring.
could
If ______________________________ Seville in the Spring.

6 It was a mistake to come to Madrid in July.
should
We ______________________________ to Madrid in July.

7 My English could be improved.
knew
I ______________________________ better.

8 I'd rather you didn't copy my homework.
wish
I ______________________________ own homework.

9 Would you like to visit the Far East?
wish
Do ______________________________ to the Far East?

10 We arrived late and missed the last bus.
only
If ______________________________ earlier; we would have caught the last bus.

5 Rewrite these sentences, beginning with the words given.

1 Mario would like a new bicycle.
Mario wishes ______________________________

2 John is not looking forward to sitting the exam on Friday.
John wishes ______________________________

3 I'm really sorry I can't come to your dinner party this evening.
I wish ______________________________

4 I was really sorry I didn't see you when you visited London last week.
I wish ______________________________

5 Mr Brown was very angry about the mess the builders made in his house.
Mr Brown wished ______________________________

6 What a pity you missed the show.
I wish ______________________________

7 It would be nice if you were here now.
I wish ______________________________

6 Rewrite these sentences, beginning with the underlined word or words.

1 I hardly ever drink whisky.

____

2 I have never been arrested by the police.

____

3 I have rarely met anyone famous.

____

4 I would not only like to go to Peru, I would also like to visit China.

____

5 I seldom make long distance telephone calls.

____

6 I will only lose weight if I start doing a sport.

____

7 I will never give up trying to get the Proficiency.

____

7 Write sentences beginning with the adverbs given and using the tenses in brackets.

1 Hardly ever ______________________________ (present simple)
2 Never ______________________________ (present perfect simple)
3 Never ______________________________ (future simple)
4 Rarely ______________________________ (present perfect simple)
5 Not only ______________________________ (would)
6 Seldom ______________________________ (present simple)
7 Only if ______________________________ (future simple)

VOCABULARY

Words often confused

1 Complete these sentences using the correct form of one of the words below in each space. Use each word more than once.

travel journey trip voyage flight excursion

1 He came home after years of foreign __________ .
2 Did you get to Athens during your __________ around Europe?
3 It's a six-hour __________ by train.
4 Columbus' __________ to India turned out very differently from what he had expected.
5 The __________ from England to India used to take six months.
6 When I go abroad, I prefer to carry __________ cheques to cash.
7 On our holiday the hotel organized lots of __________ to tourist sights.

8 That was the worst ________________ I've ever been on, there was turbulence all the way.
9 I'm going on a business ________________ to Brussels for the day.
10 We decided to break our ________________ in Oxford and spend the night there.
11 Are you going to join the ________________ to see the old castle?
12 We'll have time for a ________________ to Madrid at the weekend.
13 We made the long ________________ to Patagonia by train.
14 Our ________________ is the 406 to Rome.
15 It's lovely weather. Let's go for a day ________________ to the country.
16 I have to go to the ________________ agency to book our holiday.

Phrasal verbs

2 Match the phrasal verbs in list A with their meanings in list B.

A	B
1 take back	a manage
2 make out	b make contact
3 bring up	c fasten
4 do up	d understand
5 give back	e postpone
6 get down	f connect
7 get by	g continue
8 take up	h write what someone is saying
9 put up with	i refer to something at a meeting
10 get through	j be asked in an exam
11 cut back on	k reduce
12 go on	l organize a performance
13 put through	m start (a hobby)
14 put off	n return something
15 put on	o return something to someone
16 call off	p bear, tolerate
17 come up	q cancel

3 Complete these sentences using the correct form of one of the phrasal verbs above in each space.

1 They've ________________ the meeting because no one can go to it.
2 One thing I can't ________________ is people lying to me; I find it unacceptable.
3 I've gained a lot from this city over the years. Now I want to __________ something __________ to it.
4 Could you __________ this food __________ to the kitchen, please, and bring something fresh?
5 They're ________________ a new production of *Hamlet* at the Royal Theatre.
6 We can't afford to live like this; we'll have to ________________ our spending.
7 It's not difficult to predict the questions which are likely to ________________ in the grammar test.
8 It's scandalous – I'm going to ________________ the issue at Monday's council meeting.
9 The prime minister talked so fast that journalists found it difficult to ________________ everything he said.
10 How long can he ________________ refusing to eat and drink?

Word formation

4 Solve the clues below to complete the crossword and to find the missing word.

1 Our visit to Disneyland was simply magic. It was ________________ .
2 War is bad because it destroys. It is ________________ .
3 My best friend gives me a lot of support. She is very ________________ .
4 This ring is made of gold. It is very ________________ .
5 This water is dirty. Don't drink it, it's not ________________ .
6 The composition is a narrative but you also have to describe people and places, so it's quite ________________ .
7 The food at the hotel was so awful I couldn't eat it. It was just not ________________ .
8 Your shirt is green, yellow and blue. It's very ________________ .
9 Can you put it in the washing machine? Is it machine ________________ ?
10 The food was uncooked so I couldn't digest it. It was ________________ .
11 The book is a pleasure to read. It is very ________________ .
12 Nouns in English can be divided into those we can count and those which are ________________ .
13 She doesn't hesitate about decisions. She is very ________________ .
14 It can't be true – I don't believe it! It's ________________ !
15 He doesn't play in the attack; his role is just to defend. It's ________________ .
16 I'll never forgive your behaviour. It was absolutely ________________ .
17 The missing word is ________________ .

Answer key

UNIT 1

GRAMMAR AND USE OF ENGLISH

1 1 A 6 A 11 B
2 C 7 D 12 C
3 C 8 B 13 D
4 B 9 A 14 A
5 D 10 C 15 D

2 1 for 6 ✓ 11 will
2 all 7 has 12 ✓
3 ✓ 8 when 13 ✓
4 in 9 ✓ 14 away
5 ✓ 10 in 15 ✓

3 1 famous 6 successful
2 adolescent 7 performance
3 childhood 8 favourable
4 appearance 9 kindness
5 household 10 teenager

4 1 was telling a/his story
2 are broadcasting the Oscar ceremony
3 came up to me
4 has sold over a million
5 has been talking from
6 had never seen a cartoon
7 was she wearing
8 I had been sitting
9 and I will write
10 has only just

5 1 remember 9 refer
2 went 10 have made
3 managed 11 have seen
4 continued 12 witnessed
5 had had 13 has made
6 disappeared 14 has not become
7 have not seen 15 earns
8 has also produced

6 1 I'm finishing
2 I'll
3 They've awarded
4 They were broadcasting
5 you were wearing
6 I had been
7 I've been reading
8 I had been waiting
9 I have finished
10 I'll see

7 1 have broadcast
2 are increasing
3 had received
4 was watching, rang
5 have been watching
6 tell
7 went
8 had been snowing
9 has made
10 was raining

VOCABULARY

1

verb	adjective	noun
popularize	popular	popularity
invent	inventive	invention inventor
produce	productive	production producer
	famous	fame
create	creative	creation creator
respond	responsive	response
decide	decisive	decision
	suburban	suburb
	pleasant	pleasure
prepare		preparation
	natural	nature
originate	original	origin
	historic/al	history
appear		appearance
employ	employed	employer employee employment
translate		translation translator

2 1 suburbs 6 original
2 appears 7 produces
3 employed 8 popular
4 historic/al 9 preparation
5 translate 10 invention

3 1 come up with, make one up
2 draw up, comes up
3 took up, gave up
4 come up
5 look up
6 hold up
7 put me up
8 put up with
9 held up
10 went up

UNIT 2

GRAMMAR AND USE OF ENGLISH

1 1 C 6 D 11 A
2 A 7 C 12 A
3 A 8 B 13 B
4 A 9 D 14 A
5 A 10 B 15 D

2 1 from
2 who
3 themselves
4 have
5 often
6 their
7 although
8 have
9 up
10 been
11 can
12 too

3 1 ✓ 6 up 11 had
2 may 7 the 12 on
3 case 8 ✓ 13 ✓
4 for 9 ✓ 14 ✓
5 ✓ 10 to 15 the

4 1 chemistry
2 scientific
3 failure
4 ambitious
5 management
6 irritating
7 artistic
8 occasionally
9 particularly
10 reasonable

5 1 Do 5 Are
2 Did 6 How long
3 Does 7 What
4 Have 8 How many

1 How long 5 Is
2 Where 6 Who
3 Was 7 Do
4 What 8 Have

6 1 could you
2 haven't you
3 would you
4 don't you
5 do you
6 would you
7 didn't you

8 hadn't you
9 do they
10 shall we

8 1 If I were you (problem 4)
2 Why don't you try / You could try (problem 7)
3 Why don't you try / You could try (problem 3)
4 The best thing to do (problem 2)
5 I suggest you / You should (problem 8)
6 Why don't you try / You could try (problem 5)
7 I suggest you / You should (problem 1)
8 The best thing to do (problem 6)

VOCABULARY

1

noun	adjective
society	sociable, social
disgust	disgusting, disgusted
irritation	irritating, irritated, irritable
misery	miserable
skill	skilled, skilful
importance	important
attention	attentive
interest	interesting, interested
communication	communicative
gratitude	grateful
amusement	amusing, amused
influence	influential
despair	desperate, despairing
care	careful, caring
favour	favourite, favourable
practice	practical
accuracy	accurate
nature	natural
worry	worrying, worried
boredom	boring, bored

2 1 influential
2 worried
3 boring, bored
4 practical
5 natural
6 favourite
7 amusing
8 careful
9 grateful
10 attentive

3 1 put (me) through
2 hold on
3 turning (it) on
4 take (you) on
5 let (you) down
6 take up
7 get on
8 count on
9 go on
10 try (it) on
11 leave (it) on
12 putting on
13 set up

UNIT 3

GRAMMAR AND USE OF ENGLISH

1 1 C
2 B
3 A
4 D
5 A
6 B
7 D
8 B
9 B
10 A
11 C
12 D
13 D
14 C
15 D

2 1 you
2 ✓
3 up
4 more
5 ✓
6 a
7 long
8 from
9 ✓
10 part
11 ✓
12 to
13 it
14 was
15 ✓

3 1 suburbs
2 surroundings
3 environmental
4 industrial
5 pollution
6 disadvantage
7 entertainment
8 central
9 suitable
10 underground

4 1 are / run on time
2 is always complaining
3 share a flat with
4 is always playing
5 is getting more
6 goes perfectly with
7 turned out to be
8 is rarely in a
9 always says 'hello'
10 are always moaning

5 1 am writing
2 hope
3 wish
4 am leading
5 feel
6 have
7 takes
8 am sitting
9 looks
10 go
11 is raining
12 smell
13 is beginning
14 is staying
15 are having

6 1 is driving, comes, is coming up, crashes, shouts, didn't you put, were going, are you, answers, would have been (punchline b)
2 is driving, appears, misses, opens, shouts, opens, shouts, turns (punchline c)
3 stops, comes on, can't start, tries, change, comes up, asks (punchline a)

VOCABULARY

1

verb	noun
choose	choice
compare	comparison
complain	complaint
construct	construction
develop	development
govern	government
improve	improvement
pollute	pollution
predict	prediction
solve	solution

2 underground, ring road, motorway, motorcycle, side road, pothole, car-park, highway

3 1 motorway / highway
2 government
3 pollution
4 complaints
5 predict
6 ring road
7 construction
8 potholes
9 solution
10 side road

4 1 f
2 i
3 b, d
4 c, e
5 a, h
6 g, j

5 1 hold up
2 get back
3 take off
4 pick up
5 take off
6 pick up
7 hold up
8 get away with
9 get back
10 get away

UNIT 4

GRAMMAR AND USE OF ENGLISH

1 1 a/the 2 a 3 a/its 4 where 5 The 6 be 7 in 8 an 9 of 10 from 11 when 12 over 13 the 14 when 15 a

2 1 ✓ 2 up 3 ✓ 4 ✓ 5 them 6 our 7 ✓ 8 do 9 ✓ 10 it 11 and 12 ✓ 13 the 14 ✓ 15 ✓

3
1 surprising
2 differently
3 generally
4 northern
5 satisfactory
6 certainly
7 fairly
8 Germany
9 majority
10 exception

4
1 called my dog
2 go to/and see a film
3 to the theatre is something
4 has been in prison
5 on holiday to Italy/to Italy on holiday
6 from/in the States
7 a doctor is not
8 is still in hospital
9 go to school
10 the day and at

5 1 some 2 the 3 their 4 their 5 Ø 6 Ø 7 The 8 Ø 9 their 10 Ø 11 some/the/Ø 12 Ø 13 Ø 14 a 15 the 16 Ø

6
1 You should make small talk at parties./At parties you should make small talk.
2 You should always be on time for meetings.
3 You must not stand too close to people.
4 Eight is the luckiest number./The luckiest number is eight.
5 You must never jump the queue.
6 They avoid saying 'no' directly.
7 They often use formal titles, like 'Herr' for 'Mr'.
8 They often interrupt each other.
9 Close friends, especially women, may kiss cheeks.
10 Adults add their mother's family name to theirs.

VOCABULARY

1 **only verbs**: meet, eat
only nouns: food, lamp

1 drink 2 buy 3 turn 4 shop 5 stroll 6 order 7 visit

2

verb	noun
advertise	advertisement
appoint	appointment
arrange	arrangement
arrive	arrival
assist	assistance
direct	direction
disappear	disappearance
inform	information
introduce	introduction
know	knowledge
persuade	persuasion
refresh	refreshment

3
1 **turn back**: at the frontier, because the road was blocked
2 **turn down**: the volume, an offer, the TV, an application, the central heating
3 **turn off**: the light, the TV, the central heating, the tap, the radio
4 **turn on**: the light, the TV, the central heating, the tap, the radio
5 **turn out**: to be someone else, to be true, the light
6 **turn to**: crime, drugs
7 **turn up**: the volume, the TV, at a party, the radio, the central heating

UNIT 5

GRAMMAR AND USE OF ENGLISH

1 1 A 2 D 3 B 4 C 5 B 6 B 7 A 8 C 9 B 10 A 11 D 12 B 13 C 14 A 15 D

Answer: Stan Laurel

2 1 ✓ 2 at 3 ✓ 4 must 5 such 6 ✓ 7 ✓ 8 ✓ 9 that 10 do 11 ✓ 12 the 13 so 14 to 15 ✓

3
1 announcement
2 pleasure
3 government
4 satisfaction
5 qualifications
6 politician
7 ability
8 criminal
9 punishment
10 electricity

1 we are bankrupt.
2 it didn't happen.
3 just like the rest of us.

4
1 he was studying law
2 her father was travelling abroad
3 was not enjoying the party
4 blamed me for
5 was always misbehaving
6 a lot of acting
7 did not stop raining
8 wind was blowing
9 his arrival at
10 they were eating/having dinner they

5 1 h 2 g 3 b 4 j 5 e 6 d 7 a 8 i 9 c 10 f

6
1 was feeling
2 was wearing
3 was preparing
4 was having
5 was doing
6 was sleeping
7 was raining
8 was watching
9 was wearing
10 was going

7 (**Sample answers**)
1a I answered it.
1b I was reading.
2a They sat down.
2b They were misbehaving.
3a They were dancing.
3b They screamed.
4a I was sleeping.
4b I jumped out of the window.
5a I was watching TV.
5b I jumped up and down!

VOCABULARY

1 ***-ship***: championship, friendship, hardship, membership, partnership, scholarship
-ment: amusement, appointment, enjoyment, entertainment, excitement, management, retirement
-ness: emptiness, fondness, goodness, happiness, laziness, sadness, stinginess

2 1 stinginess
2 happiness
3 membership
4 appointment
5 excitement
6 partnership
7 entertainment
8 championship

3 1 d 2 f 3 c 4 g 5 a 6 e 7 h 8 b

5 1 takes after
2 take to
3 take it back
4 take in
5 take up
6 take five pounds off
7 took down
8 taken in

UNIT 6

GRAMMAR AND USE OF ENGLISH

1 1 or
2 front
3 other
4 each
5 when
6 only
7 our
8 in / through
9 us
10 of
11 on
12 than
13 that
14 other
15 far

2 1 out
2 ✓
3 ✓
4 yet
5 ✓
6 to
7 much
8 to
9 ✓
10 ✓
11 and
12 of
13 ✓
14 then
15 ✓

3 1 meaning
2 mainly
3 thought
4 wisdom
5 goddess
6 especially
7 sensitive
8 ability
9 immediately
10 protective

4 1 are not as clear as
2 was just as easy as
3 live as far as
4 older you get, the worse
5 is not as good as
6 is heavier than
7 are popular (as)
8 have a better
9 the most beautiful animals
10 are more loyal than

5 1 longest
2 more, than
3 more, than
4 worse
5 faster
6 no bigger
7 largest
8 more easily
9 big, as
10 much

VOCABULARY

1

verb	noun	noun (person)
act	acting, action	actor, actress
appear	appearance	
detect	detection	detective
direct	direction	director
discover	discovery	discoverer
entertain	entertainment	entertainer
examine	examination	examiner
explode	explosion	
follow		follower
immigrate	immigration	immigrant
inhabit		inhabitant
manage	management	manager
protect	protection	protector
speak	speech	speaker
understand	understanding	

There are five suffixes for people: *-or, -er, -ress, -ive, -ant*

2 1 immigrant
2 examiner
3 inhabitant
4 detective
5 discoverer
6 manager / director
7 protector
8 follower
9 speaker
10 performer / actor / actress

3 1 elephant
2 greyhound
3 giraffe
4 horse
5 eagle
6 hippopotamus
7 snake
8 ostrich
9 mosquito
10 scorpion
11 cheetah
12 whale
13 shark
14 ant
15 parrot
16 tortoise

4 1 going through
2 go on
3 go off
4 going out
5 went down
6 went up
7 going up
8 went off
9 gone down
10 going through
11 went out
12 going on
13 going up
14 gone off
15 go through
16 go on

UNIT 7

GRAMMAR AND USE OF ENGLISH

1 1 D
2 C
3 D
4 B
5 A
6 D
7 B
8 D
9 C
10 D
11 A
12 C
13 A
14 D
15 B

2 1 ✓ 6 more 11 ✓
2 the 7 ✓ 12 ✓
3 for 8 have 13 some
4 has 9 ✓ 14 been
5 ✓ 10 has 15 come

3 1 crowded
2 entertaining
3 continually
4 realistic
5 historical
6 personalities
7 admission
8 daily
9 presentations
10 nearest

4 1 has been used since / has been in use since
2 have been to Toledo
3 has been learning to drive
4 of theatres have been built
5 have been correcting these tests
6 has only just
7 have improved since
8 have been living here for
9 have been learning Spanish since
10 not gone / been to Ireland for

5 1 has closed
2 He has made
3 have seen
4 I've been reading
5 I went
6 We've sold
7 I've written
8 you've been crying
9 we've been having
10 I've been thinking

VOCABULARY

1 ***in-***: infamous, incomplete, indirect
pre-: prehistoric, preview
-al: historical, classical, musical, national
-ful: colourful, wonderful, careful

2 1 musical
2 incomplete
3 prehistoric
4 colourful
5 national
6 infamous
7 historical

3

verb	noun	adjective
dedicate	dedication	dedicated
punish	punishment	punishable
reside	residence, resident	residential
dominate	domination	dominant
repute	reputation	reputable
impress	impression	impressive
explore	exploration	exploratory
interest	interest	interested interesting
exhaust	exhaustion	exhausting exhausted
entertain	entertainment	entertaining entertained

4 1 exhausted
2 exploration
3 impression
4 reputation
5 dominates
6 residential
7 punishment

5 1 has
2 their
3 were
4 it
5 is
6 their
7 its
8 have
9 have
10 has

6 1 g 5 b
2 a 6 c
3 d 7 e
4 f

7 1 d 5 a
2 f 6 g
3 b 7 c
4 e

UNIT 8

GRAMMAR AND USE OF ENGLISH

1 1 had
2 that
3 one
4 down
5 into
6 would
7 so
8 of
9 his
10 out
11 on
12 out
13 it
14 been
15 or

2 1 ✓ 6 which 11 ✓
2 was 7 ✓ 12 ✓
3 of 8 ✓ 13 so
4 been 9 in 14 was
5 ✓ 10 had 15 ✓

3 1 failures
2 explanations
3 solution
4 specialist
5 unfinished
6 disappeared
7 journalist
8 completely
9 influential
10 reputation

4 1 he had broken into
2 had robbed his first bank / had first robbed a bank
3 had come five miles on
4 had been living in
5 because / as he had succeeded / had been successful
6 she had got married
7 Claire had turned off
8 had left the room by
9 he had been performing
10 had been driving

5 1 f 5 g
2 c 6 e
3 d 7 b
4 a

6 1 d had failed
2 e had been studying
3 a had tipped
4 h had forgotten
5 f had been travelling
6 b had come
7 c had lived
8 g had forgotten

VOCABULARY

1 1 give it back
2 take him back

3 called me back
4 look back (on the past)
5 bringing back
6 keep back
7 cut back

2

verb	adjective	noun
	curious	curiosity
	furious	fury
inform	informative	information
exaggerate	exaggerated	exaggeration
interrupt		interruption
celebrate	celebratory	celebration
object		objection
suggest		suggestion
arrive		arrival
approve	approving	approval
	gloomy	gloom
think	thoughtful thoughtless	thought
understand	understandable	understanding
	active	activity
	dangerous	danger
	mysterious	mystery
excite	excited exciting	excitement
terrify	terrifying terrified	terror

3 1 gloomy
2 mystery
3 approve
4 object
5 celebrate
6 terrifying
7 active
8 thoughtful
9 understand
10 interrupted

UNIT 9

GRAMMAR AND USE OF ENGLISH

1 1 D 2 C 3 A 4 A 5 D 6 B 7 D 8 D 9 B 10 C 11 D 12 C 13 C 14 B 15 D

2 1 for 2 ✓ 3 been 4 ✓ 5 and 6 ✓ 7 were 8 ✓ 9 have 10 about 11 ✓ 12 that 13 ✓ 14 the 15 of

3 1 willingly
2 kidnapped
3 absence
4 explanations
5 really
6 disappearance
7 spending
8 searchers
9 murdering
10 knowledge

4 1 are not allowed to leave
2 is included in
3 was accused of stealing
4 bridge has not been completed
5 will be asked to
6 is being looked into
7 going to be punished for
8 may / might have been killed
9 has been cut by
10 are not allowed to

5 (Sample answers)
1 A pensioner was run over in Banbury Road yesterday.
2 A man has been struck by lightening in a forest near Oxford.
3 A new school is going to be opened by the Mayor next week.
4 The world record for the 100 metres was broken by Tim Cater last night in Stockholm.
5 A woman was murdered at the weekend whilst on an evening stroll in Whytam Woods near Wolvercote.
6 The local hospital is going to be closed due to a lack of funds.
7 A researcher said at a conference last week that a cure for cancer will be found in the next five years.
8 English tests have been made more difficult to try to raise falling standards in English teaching.
9 A recent report in *The Times* claims that English is now spoken by one billion people.

6 1 was (it) invented
2 is called
3 is referred
4 were / have been beaten
5 are given
6 is used
7 is used
8 to be invented
9 had been invented
10 was brought
11 is built
12 are written

7 1 large, old dining
2 beautiful, antique
3 expensive, gold
4 tall, dark, handsome
5 nice, little
6 large, black, leather
7 old, blue, cotton
8 old, Indian hunting
9 stainless steel bread
10 big, fat, Chinese

VOCABULARY

1

verb	noun	adjectives
amuse	amusement	amusing amused
bore	boredom	boring bored
confuse	confusion	confusing confused
depress	depression	depressing depressed
disappoint	disappointment	disappointing disappointed
disgust	disgust	disgusting disgusted
entertain	entertainment	entertaining entertained
excite	excitement	exciting excited
exhaust	exhaustion	exhausting exhausted
fascinate	fascination	fascinating fascinated
frighten	fright	frightening frightened
involve	involvement	involving involved
irritate	irritation	irritating irritated
puzzle	puzzlement	puzzling puzzled
satisfy	satisfaction	satisfying satisfied
shock	shock	shocking shocked

2 1 pianist
2 cleaner
3 violinist
4 trainer
5 investigator
6 typist
7 directory
8 gardener
9 playwright
10 director

11 typewriter
12 smoker
13 manager
14 investigation

3 1 looking into
2 look through
3 look (them) up
4 looks down on
5 looks after
6 Look out
7 look out for
8 look back
9 looking forward to
10 look into

UNIT 10

GRAMMAR AND USE OF ENGLISH

1 1 go/went
2 have
3 to
4 into
5 than
6 get
7 their
8 or
9 been
10 example
11 have
12 as
13 and
14 from
15 if/when

2

1 ✓	6 a	11 to
2 must	7 one	12 ✓
3 many	8 had	13 off
4 it	9 about	14 them
5 ✓	10 ✓	15 ✓

3 1 personality
2 magical
3 characteristics
4 appearance
5 expression
6 confidence
7 connection
8 relationship
9 accurately
10 identical

4 1 neither the performance nor
2 only is she mean but
3 go shopping/do our shopping either at
4 only did they burgle
5 not only looks good
6 John nor I passed
7 does he want to get
8 smoke either cigarettes or
9 does he play football well
10 is either soup or salad

6

1	brought	f
2	painted	a
3	tested	i
4	repaired	e
5	cut	b
6	made	g
7	delivered	j
8	cleaned	c
9	taken	h
10	developed	d

VOCABULARY

1 1 curly
2 deep
3 turned-up
4 low
5 wavy
6 round
7 bushy
8 high

2 1 nervous
2 aggressive
3 pear-shaped
4 muscular
5 well-built
6 tense
7 insensitive
8 intelligent
9 thickset
10 self-centred
11 overweight

3 1 put (them) back
2 get (your money) back
3 hold on
4 go back on
5 go on
6 hold (me) back
7 Put on
8 get on
9 takes (me) back
10 take (you) on

UNIT 11

GRAMMAR AND USE OF ENGLISH

1

1 A	6 B	11 D
2 A	7 C	12 D
3 C	8 C	13 A
4 A	9 A	14 D
5 D	10 D	15 C

2

1 has	6 if	11 off
2 ✓	7 ✓	12 whose
3 ✓	8 it	13 the
4 to	9 ✓	14 ✓
5 a	10 ✓	15 away

3 1 dislike
2 sufficient
3 properly
4 speech
5 solution
6 effective
7 daily
8 unfortunately
9 convenient
10 consequently

4 1 was charged with
2 insisted on talking
3 apologize for having
4 we discuss the problem,
5 dark apart from
6 am tired of tidying
7 bored with
8 search for the girl went/carried
9 was very proud of
10 a lot of respect for

5

1 about	14 to
2 with	15 for
3 of	16 to
4 about	17 to
5 on	18 to
6 about	19 about
7 about	20 for
8 for	21 about
9 for	22 about
10 on	23 about
11 for	24 to
12 to	25 of
13 of	

6 **verb + preposition:** complain about, accuse of, insist on, talk about, think about, wait for, congratulate on, listen to, object to, care about, apologize for, argue about

adjective + preposition: annoyed with, anxious about, fond of, close to, loyal to, scared about, tired of
noun + preposition: admiration for, respect for, love for, threat to, solution to

VOCABULARY

1 grapefruit
mashed potatoes
strawberry
fruit salad
minced meat, minced beef
roast potatoes, roast beef
pork chop
green salad
beefburger
baked potatoes, baked beans
mineral water
instant coffee
cornflakes
French fries
ice-cream
pineapple
white wine
beetroot

2 1 peanuts
2 bananas
3 bean
4 cucumber
5 bread
6 beetroot
7 meat
8 cake

3 1 give up
2 have put on two kilos since
3 cut it up
4 have run out of milk
5 gave them away
6 put me off seeing it
7 cut down on

UNIT 12

GRAMMAR AND USE OF ENGLISH

1 1 on
2 to
3 when/if
4 is
5 or
6 this
7 from
8 go
9 a
10 real
11 however
12 type/sort/kind
13 out
14 unless
15 them

2 1 been
2 ✓
3 ✓
4 had
5 ✓
6 and
7 me
8 ✓
9 ✓
10 me
11 ✓
12 too
13 ✓
14 ✓
15 most

3 1 dreamer
2 vacation
3 enjoyable
4 unpleasant
5 successful
6 ourselves
7 impossible
8 reality
9 usually
10 awake

4 1 join you
2 had
3 was flying
4 find it
5 do not have
6 is the most
7 turned out
8 hijacked
9 have been reading
10 had
11 I am
12 Are you planning
13 has always been
14 Have you ever been

5 1 said he had not stolen
2 had ever killed
3 to know who had eaten
4 had been written before
5 he had ever dreamt
6 he had to pay
7 did you dream last
8 Katy not to work so
9 will not be late from
10 you tell me the way

6 1 Mary said it was hot.
2 Mary told us she had seen Bruce.
3 He said that he had eaten.
4 She said she had been reading a good book.
5 She claimed she could sing.
6 The doctor said I had to rest.
7 She told us she had seen him the day before.
8 She told us he had not been there that day.
9 He promised he would give me the money the next/following day.
10 He told her to go there.
11 She told him not to smoke.
12 She asked me if/whether I smoked.
13 She asked me if/whether I was coming or not.
14 She asked me where I came from.

VOCABULARY

1 1 bring out
2 bring down the price of houses
3 brought it off
4 bring back
5 bring it off
6 were you brought up
7 brought down the government
8 brought up
9 brought me back
10 bringing out

2

verb	noun	adjective
believe	belief	un/believable
create	creation	un/creative
desire	desire	un/desirable
explain	explanation	in/explicable
express	expression	un/expressive
imagine	imagination	un/imaginative imaginary
predict	prediction	un/predictable
produce	production	un/productive
	product	
punish	punishment	punishable
relate	relation relative	relative
respond	responsibility response	ir/responsible un/responsive
revolt	revolution	revolutionary
value	value	in/valuable

3 1 responsibility
2 punishment
3 creative
4 valuable
5 imaginary
6 unpredictable
7 revolution
8 expression

UNIT 13

GRAMMAR AND USE OF ENGLISH

1 1 C
2 C
3 A
4 D
5 D
6 C
7 A
8 B
9 D
10 A
11 B
12 D
13 D
14 B
15 B

2 1 also
2 ✓
3 did
4 ✓
5 then
6 ✓
7 again
8 ✓
9 up
10 at
11 too
12 ✓
13 of
14 ✓
15 ✓

3 1 guilty
2 unemployed
3 investigators
4 resident
5 destination
6 desperately
7 employers
8 explanation
9 lawyer
10 criminal

4 1 I knew whose car this
2 am not used to driving
3 did not use to watch
4 a habit of disappearing
5 in a neighborhood that/which
6 did not use to smoke
7 cannot get used to
8 we would go to
9 am getting used to learning
10 where I used to go

VOCABULARY

1 1 which = blackmail
2 which = hijack
3 who = mugger
4 where, who = prison
5 where = cell
6 which = fine
7 which = murder
8 which = arson
9 who = culprit
10 who = criminal
11 whose = detective
12 whose = guard
13 where = station
14 who = squad
15 which = beat
16 who = jury
17 whose = lawyer
18 where = court
19 where = dock
20 which = evidence

2 1 lawyer
2 evidence
3 hijack
4 guard
5 blackmail
6 jury
7 mugger
8 station
9 fine
10 culprit

3

verb	noun
accuse	accusation
appear	appearance
assassinate	assassination
commit	commitment
confirm	confirmation
educate	education
encourage	encouragement
impress	impression
imprison	imprisonment
improve	improvement
invest	investment
occur	occurence
participate	participation
produce	production
prosecute	prosecution
punish	punishment
receive	reception
rob	robbery
select	selection
suspect	suspicion

4 1 encouragement
2 commit
3 robbery
4 occur
5 appearance
6 assassination
7 punishment, imprisonment
8 Education
9 Participation
10 improve

5 1 made up
2 take up
3 make out
4 taken out
5 make for
6 made off
7 took off
8 made up
9 took (you) for
10 took (me) out
11 made out
12 made up

UNIT 14

GRAMMAR AND USE OF ENGLISH

1 1 with
2 on
3 between
4 will
5 the
6 about
7 which
8 of
9 how
10 only
11 into
12 by
13 whose
14 whom
15 has

2 1 a
2 being
3 ✓
4 to
5 ✓
6 about
7 ✓
8 which
9 ✓
10 who
11 the
12 of
13 on
14 ✓
15 ✓

3 1 education
2 backgrounds
3 suburban
4 poverty
5 entertainment
6 activities
7 fewer
8 Commercials
9 favourite
10 violent

4 1 cannot afford to buy
2 suggested staying in and watching
3 did not remember to post
4 will always remember lying
5 have stopped speaking
6 I stopped to talk
7 regret (to say) that you
8 regret not marrying
9 could hear people talking
10 you try to make

5 1 avoid
2 afford
3 can't stand
4 Would (you) mind

5 planned / decided
6 love / like / enjoy
7 forgot
8 suggest / start
9 worth
10 Would (you) like

6 1 reading
2 to come
3 to have
4 hearing
5 reading
6 to learn
7 to see
8 to ask
9 to travel
10 to arrive
11 to make
12 hearing

7 1 can
2 should
3 will / would
4 could / should
5 can
6 should
7 will
8 could

8 1 does
2 has
3 am
4 didn't
5 Haven't
6 do
7 has
8 be

VOCABULARY

1 a channel
b broadcast
c edition
d box office
e article
f quiz
g column

2 1 switch
2 soap
3 channel
4 episode
5 comedy
6 cartoon
7 series
8 audience
9 viewers
10 volume

3

noun	adjective
athletic	athletic
care	careful
centre	central
comedy	comical
danger	dangerous
drama	dramatic
education	educational
environment	environmental
experiment	experimental
harm	harmful
history	historic / al
humour	humorous
origin	original
poison	poisonous
practice	practical
science	scientific
tradition	traditional
use	useful

4 1 poisonous
2 scientific
3 harmful
4 educational
5 environmental
6 dramatic / historic / al
7 careful
8 humourous
9 athletic
10 original

5 1 change
2 warm
3 still
4 awake
5 diary
6 word
7 on
8 secret
9 back
10 up
11 on
12 off

UNIT 15

GRAMMAR AND USE OF ENGLISH

1 1 B
2 D
3 A
4 C
5 B
6 C
7 A
8 C
9 D
10 B
11 D
12 A
13 B
14 A
15 C

2 1 though
2 ✓
3 been
4 that
5 ✓
6 do
7 to
8 and
9 at
10 ✓
11 ✓
12 will
13 ✓
14 has
15 ✓

3 1 ignorance
2 unbelievable
3 knowledge
4 third
5 expressions
6 understanding
7 accurately
8 loaves
9 confidence
10 unable

4 1 going to go on
2 (it) will be colder
3 I am having my
4 takes off at
5 is going to
6 we will have
7 will lay the table
8 you doing anything
9 match kicks off / starts / begins at
10 is looking after

5 1 I'm going
2 I'm leaving
3 I'm going to
4 starts
5 I'll see
6 You're going to break
7 I'll lend

6 1 f
2 c
3 h
4 b
5 g
6 d
7 a
8 e

VOCABULARY

1

verb	noun
arrive	arrival
believe	belief
celebrate	celebration
conclude	conclusion
decide	decision
depart	departure
describe	description
dominate	domination
enquire	enquiry
examine	examination
exist	existence
inform	information
invent	invention
invite	invitation
know	knowledge
predict	prediction
promote	promotion
publish	publication

2 1 knowledge of computers is very
2 is the departure of the
3 arrival someone will be there to meet him
4 (the) information to the police
5 is the publication of his
6 a description of the
7 received / had an invitation
8 was an invention of Bell's

3 1 f 5 h
2 i 6 a
3 g 7 d, e
4 j 8 b, c

4 1 took to
2 take (you) on
3 take on
4 take up
5 take up
6 take (it) back
7 give up
8 is picking up
9 looks up to
10 gone up

UNIT 16

GRAMMAR AND USE OF ENGLISH

1 1 when
2 towards
3 of
4 only
5 the
6 a / one
7 when / how
8 it
9 others
10 at
11 not
12 to
13 some
14 have
15 their

2 1 belief
2 proof
3 beings
4 superstitious
5 explanations
6 knowledge
7 reasonable
8 influential
9 travellers
10 anxious

3 1 it rains, we stay at
2 (you should) refuse to answer them
3 buy a new suit if
4 I could I would
5 were you, I would
6 this button, the light comes
7 for money, (you should) ignore
8 you want you relax, you
9 broke that vase, you would
10 does not get better

4 1 f 6 d
2 i 7 e
3 b 8 j
4 a 9 c
5 g 10 h

VOCABULARY

1

number	words
12	twelve
12th	twelfth
13th	thirteenth
22	twenty-second
1/2	half
1/4	a quarter
75th	seventy-fifth
3/4	three-quarters
610	six hundred and ten
250 000	two hundred and fifty thousand
2 000 000	two million
8 August 1951	the eighth of August, nineteen fifty-one
1 May	the first of May
30/9/98	the thirtieth of September, nineteen ninety-eight
100%	one hundred per cent
25 x 25 =	twenty-five times twenty-five equals
150 ÷ 5 =	a / one hundred and fifty divided by five equals
34 – 6 =	thirty-four minus six equals

2 1 First 5 Half
2 eleventh 6 three
3 second 7 one
4 Third 8 two

3 1 hurt
2 harm
3 break, smash, damage
4 crashed
5 broke
6 destroyed
7 demolish
8 injured
9 sprained
10 crack

4 **make:** the beds, an attempt, a cake, friends, war, dinner, a decision, money
do: the washing up, housework, nothing, a lot of work, the shopping, well, your best
go: swimming, for a walk, skiing, shopping, on holiday
have: a baby, a swim, a try, a go, a lot of work, dinner, friends, nothing, money

5 1 go ahead
2 done up
3 made (herself) up
4 gone by
5 make of
6 had (a tooth) out
7 had (my pyjamas) on
8 do up

UNIT 17

GRAMMAR AND USE OF ENGLISH

1 1 C 6 B 11 A
2 B 7 A 12 B
3 A 8 C 13 D
4 B 9 D 14 C
5 D 10 D 15 A

2 1 by 6 to 11 ✓
2 ✓ 7 like 12 very
3 ✓ 8 ✓ 13 for
4 then 9 done 14 ✓
5 ✓ 10 are 15 as

3 1 realistic
2 complaint
3 argument
4 better
5 artist
6 admiringly
7 unable
8 cheating
9 conclusion
10 life-like

4 1 must not wear jeans
2 do not have to
3 need to wear smarter
4 did not let us wear
5 must not get up
6 had to have

7 we need to bring
8 need not have got
9 are not allowed to
10 do not need to buy / need not buy

5 1 You do not have to have talent to paint as a hobby.
2 You need not / do not need to be a successful painter.
3 We did not have to do music at school.
4 You do not have to practise a lot to play the piano well.
5 You need / need to have a loud voice to be an actor.
6 You do not need to be tall to be a successful actor.
7 Michaelangelo did not need to go to art school to learn how to paint.

VOCABULARY

1

verb	noun	C or U?
advertise	advertisement	C
grow	growth	C & U
produce	production	C & U
	product	C
televise	television	C & U
explain	explanation	C
consume	consumption	U
free	freedom	U
invent	invention	C & U
enjoy	enjoyment	U
equip	equipment	U
suggest	suggestion	C
inform	information	U
behave	behaviour	U
confide	confidence	C & U
publicize	publicity	U

2 1 freedom
2 confidence
3 behaviour
4 information
5 equipment
6 enjoyment
7 explanation

3 **countable nouns:** brush, frame, painter, exhibition, gallery, masterpiece

4 1 any
2 much, a bit
3 some
4 a great deal of
5 enough
6 little
7 more
8 any

5 1 h
2 e
3 i
4 c
5 a
6 d
7 j
8 b
9 g
10 f

6 1 let (the secret) out
2 saw (him) off
3 ran into
4 looking into
5 run out
6 lets (you) down
7 broken down
8 saw through
9 broke off
10 look out

UNIT 18

GRAMMAR AND USE OF ENGLISH

1 1 of
2 in
3 was
4 as
5 at
6 was
7 between
8 before / previously
9 their
10 by
11 which
12 The
13 not
14 spend
15 at

2 1 powerful
2 valuable
3 unseen
4 spacecraft
5 hidden
6 successful
7 exploration
8 headquarters
9 measurements
10 distance

3 1 we will be lying
2 will have been working
3 we will have been married
4 will be doing a test
5 I will have written
6 will not be using
7 will have been built
8 I will be going
9 will be working all evening
10 will have cut down

4 1 will be getting
2 will (you) be going
3 will (I) be going
4 will have been
5 will have gone
6 will be sitting
7 will not be strolling
8 will be carrying
9 will have written
10 will have typed
11 will have been sweating
12 will be travelling
13 will have interviewed
14 will (you) be leaving
15 will be catching

5 1 will have increased
2 will be speaking
3 will have grown
4 will have found
5 will have replaced
6 will have given up
7 will be receiving
8 will be flying
9 will have stopped
10 will be going

VOCABULARY

1

verb	noun
accomodate	accomodation
assist	assistance
believe	belief
choose	choice
combine	combination
complete	completion
conclude	conclusion
connect	connection
correct	correction
declare	declaration
differ	difference
explain	explanation
express	expression
imagine	imagination
introduce	introduction
investigate	investigation
populate	population
publish	publication
receive	reception
register	registration
relate	relation, relative
revolve	revolution
save	savings
speak	speech
suggest	suggestion

2 1 combination
2 registration
3 population
4 expression
5 accomodation
6 relation / relative
7 savings
8 reception
9 correction
10 difference

3 1 employer
2 publisher
3 director
4 traveller
5 astronaut
6 manager
7 explorer
8 cameraman
9 plumber
10 chef
11 judge
12 reporter
13 photographer

4

1 j	7 i
2 f	8 c
3 g	9 a
4 k	10 e
5 b	11 d
6 h	

5 1 get around
2 get (his message) across
3 get ahead
4 get along
5 got round
6 get at
7 get away
8 get off

UNIT 19

GRAMMAR AND USE OF ENGLISH

1

1 B	6 A	11 B
2 C	7 D	12 D
3 D	8 C	13 B
4 C	9 A	14 D
5 B	10 C	15 A

2

1 ✓	6 ✓	11 still
2 being	7 ✓	12 ✓
3 out	8 will	13 in
4 ✓	9 more	14 good
5 some	10 for	15 ✓

3 1 gambling
2 winning
3 harmless
4 Unlucky
5 amusing
6 beginner's
7 fascinating
8 boring
9 unfortunately
10 addiction

4 1 would have had a nice
2 if it was not so
3 had not gone to bed late,
4 will not win any money
5 not been driving so fast,
6 you arrive, please give
7 would have been
8 would not be taking / would not have to take
9 I would get married
10 not have lost so much

5 1 f
2 a
3 i
4 g
5 b
6 d
7 j
8 c
9 e
10 h

6 1 can't have drowned
2 can't have been stabbed
3 can't have been shot
4 could not have killed
5 might have had
7 could not have killed
8 must have commited
9 must / might have poisoned

VOCABULARY

1 1 withdraw
2 newsagent
3 expensive
4 platform
5 registered
6 account
7 fishmonger
8 check-out
9 invaluable
10 cost
11 store
12 stationer
13 floors
14 trolley
15 dear
16 department store

2 shop assistant, department store, newsagent, post office, postcard, youth hostel, travel agent, credit card, shoe shop, luxury goods, junk food, pocket money

3 1 shop assistant
2 travel agent
3 youth hostel
4 department store
5 post office
6 luxury goods
7 pocket money

4 1 b, f
2 j
3 a
4 e
5 c, d
6 g
7 i
8 h

5 1 get ahead
2 got round
3 get down
4 get through
5 get off
6 get over
7 gets (me) down
8 get round
9 get down to
10 get by

UNIT 20

GRAMMAR AND USE OF ENGLISH

1 1 as
2 are
3 In
4 most
5 of
6 it
7 Before
8 but / although
9 or
10 which
11 out
12 when
13 will

14 not
15 their

2 1 such 2 have 3 it 4 ✓ 5 one 6 ✓ 7 much 8 up 9 if 10 ✓ 11 which 12 of 13 ✓ 14 we 15 ✓

3 1 inexpensive
2 international
3 roughly
4 Italian
5 household
6 successfully
7 Musicals
8 fashionable
9 speciality
10 untouched

4 1 must be very tired
2 promised not to come home
3 should not have gone
4 let us stay up late
5 warned them not to
6 were made to do
7 rather read books than
8 when I hear birds singing
9 general ordered the soldiers to
10 I felt an insect crawling

5 1 to hear
2 be
3 tell
4 to have
5 to stay
6 check
7 to begin
8 to do
9 to hire
10 get
11 to visit
12 to go
13 book
14 recommend
15 to ask

6 1 lying
2 lending
3 walking
4 laughing
5 Cooking
6 complaining
7 playing
8 hearing
9 having
10 meeting

VOCABULARY

1 1 spend
2 kind
3 tap
4 serve
5 train
6 case
7 fall
8 way
9 odd
10 rock

4 1 came across
2 turn up
3 keep up
4 put forward
5 cutting down on
6 make out
7 put up with
8 put out
9 put on
10 took me on

UNIT 21

GRAMMAR AND USE OF ENGLISH

1 1 C 2 D 3 A 4 B 5 A 6 C 7 D 8 B 9 A 10 D 11 A 12 C 13 C 14 A 15 D

2 1 ✓ 2 to 3 will 4 enough 5 ✓ 6 such 7 going 8 ✓ 9 of 10 ✓ 11 it 12 ✓ 13 he 14 ✓ 15 up

3 1 basically
2 majority
3 sponsorship
4 advertising
5 commercials
6 equipment
7 particularly
8 disappointing
9 ridiculous
10 personalities

4 1 have had a nap
2 soon as the police arrived
3 you have finished eating
4 moment the players appeared
5 the time we got
6 have to wait / stay until John
7 went straight home after
8 you have given it a
9 unless you have had enough
10 ring when I get back

5 1 Take your umbrella with you in case it rains.
2 You can go to the party as long as you come back by midnight.
3 As soon as she heard the news, she telephoned her mother.
4 I wish I knew Spanish.
5 Read the instructions before switching / you switch the machine on.
6 Do not stop working / work until you have finished the task.
7 It is time we left.
8 When I have enough money, I will buy that car.

6 1 Firstly
2 in spite of
3 However
4 Not only, but also
5 What's more
6 In addition
7 Finally
8 even though
9 As for
10 to sum up

VOCABULARY

1 1 scene / seen
2 rays / raise
3 wait / weight
4 heir / air
5 sight / site
6 flu / flew
7 plain / plane
8 tires / tyres
9 allowed / aloud
10 fare / fair

2 1 Take
2 is
3 This
4 five
5 many
6 the
7 your
8 all
9 first
10 spends

11 good
12 wasting
13 one
14 from
15 At
16 pass
17 half
18 table
19 tell
20 on

3 1 fallen out
2 join in
3 join up
4 kick off
5 kick (him) out
6 playing up
7 drop out
8 catch on
9 catch up
10 fallen (too far) behind
11 send (him) off
12 send (him) up
13 drop (me) off
14 play away

UNIT 22

GRAMMAR AND USE OF ENGLISH

1 1 where
2 because
3 at
4 out
5 for
6 All
7 of
8 ago
9 there
10 which
11 Apart
12 hardly
13 it
14 when
15 us

2 1 who
2 ✓
3 that
4 a
5 it
6 ✓
7 ✓
8 that
9 have
10 ✓
11 already
12 I
13 to
14 ✓
15 except

3 1 stressful
2 surprising
3 successful
4 preparation
5 endless
6 Flying
7 unfamiliar
8 knowledge
9 helpless
10 waiter

4 1 only we had gone to
2 should have chosen
3 wish I had gone to
4 wish Tenerife had not been
5 only I could visit
6 should not have come
7 wish I knew English
8 wish you would do your
9 you wish to go
10 only we had arrived

5 1 Mario wishes he had a new bicycle.
2 John wishes he did not have to sit/he were not sitting the exam on Friday.
3 I wish I could come to your dinner party this evening, but I cannot.
4 I wish I had seen you when you visited London last week.
5 Mr Brown wished the builders had not made the/such a mess in his house.
6 I wish you had seen the show.
7 I wish you were here now.

6 1 Hardly ever do I drink whisky.
2 Never have I been arrested by the police.
3 Rarely have I met anyone famous.
4 Not only would I like to go to Peru, I would also like to visit China.
5 Seldom do I make long distance telephone calls.
6 Only if I start doing a sport will I lose weight.
7 Never will I give up trying to get the Proficiency.

VOCABULARY

1 1 travel
2 trip
3 journey
4 voyage
5 journey/voyage
6 traveller's
7 excursions
8 flight
9 trip
10 journey
11 excursion
12 trip
13 journey
14 flight
15 trip
16 travel

2 1 n
2 d
3 i
4 c
5 o
6 h
7 a
8 m
9 p
10 b
11 k
12 g
13 f
14 e
15 l
16 q
17 j

3 1 put off/called off
2 put up with
3 give (something) back
4 take (this food) back
5 putting on
6 cut back on
7 come up
8 bring up
9 get down
10 go on

4 1 magical
2 destructive
3 supportive
4 valuable
5 drinkable
6 descriptive
7 edible
8 colourful
9 washable
10 indigestible
11 readable
12 uncountable
13 decisive
14 unbelievable
15 defensive
16 unforgiveable
17 misunderstanding